6·99

The
Connell Guide
to
Thomas Hardy's

———

Tess of the d'Urbervilles

———

by
Cedric Watts &
Jolyon Connell

Contents

How convincing is the climax of *Tess*? 100

Did a President of the Immortals
sport with Tess? 105

What does *Tess* tell us about human
consciousness? 116

NOTES

Introduction

Few novels have caused more of a stir than *Tess of the d'Urbervilles*. On December 5, 1892, just over a year after it was published, Robert Louis Stevenson wrote to Henry James, declaring *Tess* "damnable": "one of the worst, weakest, least sane, most *voulu* [i.e. forced] books I have yet read". James responded in kind:

> I am meek and ashamed where the public clatter is deafening – so I bowed my head and let "Tess of the D's" pass. But oh yes, dear Louis, she is vile. The pretence of "sexuality" is only equalled by the absence of it, and the abomination of the language by the author's reputation for style. There are indeed some pretty smells and sights and sounds. But you have better ones in Polynesia.

Hardy thereafter referred to James and Stevenson, these "good-natured friends" of his, as "the Polonius and the Osric* of novelists". On the other side of the Atlantic, W. P. Trent, in the *Sewanee Review*, said that "everyone is reading or has read the book":

> "How horrible, how pessimistic," exclaims one reader. "How absurd," says another, "to attempt to

---

* Shakespeare's two dim-witted characters in *Hamlet*.

prove that such a woman was pure" [...] "What is the good of such stories when they only make one weep?" says a third. "It is the greatest tragedy of modern times," says a fourth. "It is a dangerous book to put into the hands of the young," says a fifth. And so on through a chorus of praise and blame...

In England, the Duchess of Abercorn stated that she divided her dinner-guests according to their view of Tess. If they deemed her "a little harlot", she put them in one group; if they said "Poor wronged innocent!", she put them in another. It is a telling illustration of the novel's word-of-mouth success. The *Daily News* wittily claimed that "pessimism (we had almost said Tessimism) is popular and fashionable". Fan-mail arrived: Hardy said that his mail from readers even included even confessional letters from various wives who, like Tess, had gained premarital sexual experience but, unlike her, had not told their husbands of it.

Hardy's fame was now so great that he was a frequent guest at fashionable dinner parties. In 1892 he recorded that *Tess*'s fame had spread round the world and that translations were multiplying, "its publication in Russia exciting great interest". Controversy generated publicity. Publicity generated prosperity.

Sales of *Tess* far surpassed those of any of

Hardy's previous works. R. G. Cox reports:

> Of the three-volume edition of "Tess" two further
> impressions of 500 each had succeeded the first
> 1,000 within four months. The one-volume reprint
> at 6s [six shillings] ran to five impressions totalling
> 17,000 between September 1892 and the end of the
> year.

The novel was soon translated into French,
German, Dutch, Italian, Polish and Russian,
and between 1900 and 1930 was reprinted "some
forty times in England alone". (Macmillan
published 226,750 copies between 1895 and
1929.)

In addition to making Hardy famous and rich,
the scandalous *Tess* attracted, and has continued
to attract, an extraordinary range of critical
opinion. Victorian reviewers, humanists, neo-
Marxists, deconstructionists, cultural materialists,
new historicists: everyone has had something to
say about the novel. This book, drawing on the best
of these critics, will attempt to show why, for all its
faults, it has such power, and to explain the angry
and uncompromising vision of the world contained
within its pages.

A summary of the plot

Tess Durbeyfield is one of nine children of two poor villagers in Blackmoor Vale in the south of England. Her father, feckless and inclined to drunkenness, is rendered lazier by the information that he is a descendant of the noble family, the d'Urbervilles. Tess, trying to help him, feels responsible for an accident which results in the death of his horse, Prince. Pressed by her mother, she approaches and "claims kin" with a Mrs d'Urberville who lives nearby. She and her son Alec, however, are not really relations at all: the family has annexed the name "d'Urberville", having originally been called "Stoke".

Tess goes to work for Mrs d'Urberville. The sensual Alec is attracted to Tess and strives to seduce her. At first she resists him, but eventually, after being rescued from a potentially dangerous brawl, she is overcome late one night. Afterwards, she becomes his mistress for some weeks, then leaves him. She gives birth to his child, who dies after an improvised baptism.

She leaves home to work as a dairy-maid on a fertile farm, and becomes engaged to Angel Clare, a clergyman's son who apparently holds liberal views. On their wedding night, Angel confesses to a sexual liaison in his past, and is forgiven by Tess; but when she tells him of her affair with Alec, he is horrified and leaves her. She returns to her family (which becomes increasingly needy), and subsequently toils in harsh conditions on a bleak farm where she is cruelly victimised by the farmer, who had once been assaulted by Angel. Alec, influenced by Angel's devout father, has become a preacher, but, on encountering Tess by chance, is again strongly attracted to her, abandons his piety, and wins her back. Angel, who has travelled to South America, has not responded to her written pleas, and Alec is able to provide financial help for her family. Reluctantly, therefore, Tess again becomes Alec's mistress.

Angel returns penitently from Brazil, seeks Tess, and finds her living with Alec. There follows an altercation between Alec and Tess; Tess stabs Alec to death, and flees with Angel. The fugitives enjoy a brief idyll in the New Forest. When they reach Stonehenge, Tess is arrested; and later, at a prison in Wintoncester, she is hanged. Angel now has a new companion, Tess's younger sister 'Liza-Lu, who had been commended to him by Tess herself.

Poster for Roman Polanski's 1979 film Tess, *with the 18-year-old Nastassja Kinski n the title role*

NASTASSJA KINSKI

Tess

EIN FILM VON
ROMAN POLANSKI

mit PETER FIRTH LEIGH LAWSON

und JOHN COLLIN · DAVID MARKHAM · ROSEMARY MARTIN · RICHARD PEARSON · CAROLYN PICKLES · PASCALE DE BOYSSON

GERARD BRACH · ROMAN POLANSKI · JOHN BROWNJOHN   GEOFFREY UNSWORTH bvc und GHISLAIN CLOQUET afcc

What is *Tess of the d'Urbervilles* about?

Tess of the d'Urbervilles marks a turning point in Hardy's life. When it was published, he was already a well-established and successful novelist, and though such earlier novels as *Desperate Remedies* and *The Woodlanders* had caused some controversy, Hardy had claimed that the views expressed in them were not necessarily his own. Indeed, as the critic Penny Boumelha has pointed out, he even denied he had any personal views *at all* on the subjects he wrote about. His Preface to *The Woodlanders*, for example, essentially disguises his real (liberal) views on divorce. With the writing of *Tess*, however, this changed: "Hardy's elaborately constructed, resolutely

WHAT'S IN A NAME?

What's in a name? Plenty, when Hardy is choosing it. The nickname "Tess" is a familiar abbreviation of "Teresa", name of the 16th-century saint whose ecstatic trance was famously sculpted by Bernini. The title's reference to her as Tess "of the D'Urbervilles", or subsequently "of the d'Urbervilles", rather than as Tess "Durbeyfield", heralds the theme of the decline of her family from its aristocratic past. The surname "d'Urberville" has a range of meanings: French *d'*, of, from; Latin *urbs*, city; French *urbain,* urban; Latin

non-controversial public persona," says Boumelha, began to break down.

It wasn't so much the plot that caused the fuss – other fictional heroines, after all, had "fallen" (Hetty Sorrel in George Eliot's *Adam Bede* being one). It was the new polemical framework Hardy gave to his story. In few works of fiction is the author's central purpose made as plain as it is in *Tess*. Beneath his restrained public persona, Hardy had always been a passionate moralist, but now he was keen to pick a fight. In his "Explanatory Note" to the first edition (1891), he provocatively claims to have represented in the novel "what everybody nowadays thinks and feels", while *Tess*'s aggressive subtitle, "A Pure Woman", makes the point even plainer, with its pre-emptive challenge to any conventional or puritanical reader who might

---

villa, country-house, farm; French *ville*, town, city. The suffix's shift from "ville" to "field" stresses the rural situation of the declining family.

Hardy liked to trace his own ancestry through the centuries, claiming descent from the "le Hardys" of Jersey, and considered restoring the "le" to his name. His ancestors, he said, included the Captain

Thomas Hardy who famously comforted the dying Admiral Nelson on the flagship *Victory* at the Battle of Trafalgar. "The decline and fall of the Hardys much in evidence hereabout," the author ruefully recorded in his journal in 1888, adding: "So we go down, down, down"; and *Tess*, Chapter 19, cites the Hardys' decline.◆

damn Tess for her behaviour.

In writing *Tess*, Hardy, like Swift, was "lacerated by fierce indignation", and the result is what the critic Trevor Johnson calls "a noble and tragic book informed by a rage of pity not for Tess alone but for all mankind". Hardy assails not only the Victorian notion that virginity should outweigh other considerations in assessing a woman's character, but also the notorious sexual "double standard" whereby it was deemed natural and forgivable for a man to "sow his wild oats" but disgraceful and irredeemable for a woman to lose her virginity before marriage. Hardy was well aware of the outrage he would cause, and in his Note to the first edition he craftily cited Saint Jerome's declaration: "If an offence come out of the truth, better is it that the offence come than that the truth be concealed." In a new edition, a

THE TITLE

Like the novel as a whole, its very title evolved. An early version, "The Body and Soul of Sue", gave way to "Too Late Beloved" (properly "Too Late, Belovèd!"), borrowing a phrase from Shelley's love-poem "Epipsychidion". That phrase could apply to the heroine's love-relationship and marriage to Angel, or, more tellingly, to his tardy return to her after his Brazilian travels. "Epipsychidion", one of Hardy's favourite poems, is cited with admiration by Sue

year later, he specifically challenged objectors to the adjective "pure", declaring:

> They ignore the meaning of the word in Nature, together with all æsthetic claims upon it, not to mention the spiritual interpretation afforded by the finest side of their own Christianity.

He implies that Tess remains "a pure woman" in two important senses: "an unadulterated instance of womanhood"; and "a woman who either is essentially unsullied, being the victim, or, if tainted by volition, has good motives (e.g. helping her family) and has regained virtue by penitence". When referring to the "the finest side of their own Christianity", Hardy is almost certainly thinking of John 8: 3-11. To the argument that the woman "taken in adultery" should be stoned to death,

---

Bridehead in the later novel, *Jude the Obscure*. The poem offered the controversial doctrine that some ardent people were suited not to monogamy but to diverse love-relationships. Hardy's sympathy with this doctrine understandably annoyed his first wife, who (probably recalling oriental harems) recoiled from his "Eastern" orientation. Another title-possibility considered by the author was "A Daughter of the D'Urbervilles". The prominent name of Tess herself in the final title establishes that the work belongs to the tradition of the *Bildungsroman* – a German term meaning "novel concerning a person's education and development".◆

Jesus said: "He that is without sin among you, let him first cast a stone at her"; and, when nobody volunteered, Jesus told the woman to depart and sin no more.

The novel repeatedly emphasises the importance of good intentions, particularly Tess's, even when her later deeds don't match them. Reflecting this view, Hardy told an interviewer in August 1892: "I still maintain that her innate purity remained intact to the very last; though I frankly own that a certain outward purity left her on her last fall." (By "last fall" he means her second term as Alec's mistress.)

But the use of the word "pure" has continued to try the patience of some critics. In 1978, Mary Jacobus severely commented: "To invoke purity in connection with a career that includes not simply seduction, but collapse into kept woman and murderess, taxes the linguistic resources of the most permissive conventional moralist." The idea of Tess's purity, said Jacobus, like the sub-title "A Pure Woman", had been "stuck on" by Hardy to meet objections which the novel encountered before first publication. Even Hardy himself, in the end, had second thoughts about that sub-title. "*Melius fuerat non scribere* [it would have been better not to write it]," he ruefully remarked in 1912.

The arguments about the sub-title are symptomatic of the wider critical battle which has long been fought over *Tess* and indeed over Hardy's fiction in general. Several early reviewers of the novel disliked it – not just the subject matter, which they found distasteful, but also some of the sexual descriptive material, which they found all too frank. Some 20th-century critics echoed these complaints. And while earlier novels had been attacked on similar grounds, the personal element in *Tess* gave a new twist to the criticism.

Hardy's close identification with his heroine, and the way he seems actively to plot against her, has troubled many critics. The influential F. R. Leavis, for example, approved Henry James's damning verdict of *Tess*, loftily dismissing its author as a "provincial manufacturer of gauche and heavy fictions that sometimes have corresponding virtues". Earlier heroines, like Bathsheba Everdene in *Far from the Madding Crowd*, and Eustacia Vye in *The Return of the Native*, are portrayed more objectively: Bathsheba, for instance – peeved because Farmer Boldwood is ignoring her – mischievously sends him a valentine after tossing a hymn book to decide his fate. Hardy views this with a cold eye, yet we warm to the bold, wilful Bathsheba, for all her faults, as we do to the passionate Eustacia, who wants to be "loved to madness", because, for all the occasional clumsiness in the narratives of these novels, the characters seem so real. With *Tess* this coolness of view has gone, and while it is an extraordinarily vivid and passionate novel it is also an uneven one: Hardy's consciousness is so close to Tess's – as it is to the consciousness of the hopelessly poor would-be scholar, Jude, in his last novel – that it puts a great strain on his art.

Yet if some critics have never warmed to Hardy, most acknowledge that *Tess* has an extraordinary power. The intense rage he feels on his heroine's behalf gives it a unique passion. As the final lines about the "President of the Immortals" (59)* suggest, that rage extends beyond Tess herself, and her victimisation by Victorian double standards, to encompass a more general anger about the plight of women and suffering humanity in general. The themes Hardy develops in *Tess* flow from his pessimistic view of life: the isolation of the individual; the subjectivity of experience; the tendency of lovers to idealise the objects of their love; the unlikeliness of happiness in human relationships; the destructiveness of the sexual instinct and its association with death; and the brutal and unforgiving way in which events may happen, suggestive of some kind of malignant force at work behind creation. The "accidentalism" in Hardy's novels, says the American critic Dorothy Van Ghent, is "not itself accidental". On the earth,

Throughout this book, the numbers in brackets refer to the chapters from which quotations are taken

as seen by Hardy, accident and coincidence constitute order.

> In the accidentalism of Hardy's universe we can recognize the profound truth of the darkness in which life is cast, darkness both within the soul and without...

It is not just society which crushes Tess: it is society and nature, working together. Society is only what another highly sympathetic critic, Tony Tanner, calls "a functioning part of a larger process". The policemen who come to arrest Tess at the end appear as the sun rises over Stonehenge. Tess "is a sacrifice to both". Hardy's universe, says Tanner, is one "of radical opposition, working to destroy what it works to create, crushing to death what it coaxes into life".

Throughout his novels, and especially in *Tess* and the novel which followed it, *Jude the Obscure*, Hardy suggests that the sensitive individual can never feel at home in the world. Tess herself feels that her mind can drift away from her body, and, towards the end, hardly recognizes her body as her own. The intelligent consciousness, in Hardy's view, always feels apart and is likely to suffer and to share the feeling of Sue Bridehead in *Jude*, that ultimately we must blame the universe "and things in general – they're so nasty and cruel".

Does Hardy make us feel Tess is doomed from the start?

Hardy was brilliant at starting a novel. *The Mayor of Casterbridge*, for example, memorably opens with the hero, Michael Henchard, selling his wife to a sailor at a village fair. But while *The Mayor of Casterbridge* then has to slow down to lay the basis for the narrative that follows, the opening of *Tess*, by contrast, as Michael Irwin says in his introduction to the Wordsworth edition, is "brilliantly contrived to initiate a sequence".

The early chapters rapidly traverse the events leading to Tess's pregnancy. They move the

HARDY'S REVISIONS

In the course of revising the text over the years, Hardy made numerous small but significant changes. Some of them complicated Tess's feelings towards Alec, introducing an element of "confused surrender" (12) in her relationship with him. Alec was made more cynical. For example: in the text of 1891, he says that Christian belief came to him "like a shining light"; but, in the text of 1912, he says it came "like a jolly new idea" (45). Other changes made Angel Clare slightly less unsympathetic than he had been in 1891. Then, when rebuking Tess, he had declared: "You are an unapprehending peasant woman"; but by 1912 the words were: "You almost

narrative along at an exhilarating pace, in a series of logical steps, illustrating Hardy's view that tragedy can derive from the most trivial of causes. They also establish the importance of class in the novel, and the extent to which Tess is shaped by ancestry as well as poverty.

Romantic and sexual relationships transgressing social boundaries are at the core of Hardy's fiction, as Penny Boumelha has noted; significantly, his first (unpublished and subsequently lost) novel was called *The Poor Man and the Lady*. In early novels like *Far from the Madding Crowd* and *Under the Greenwood Tree*, such differences are resolved to produce more or less happy endings. But, in the later works, as Boumelha says, the differences are preserved "in all

make me say you are an unapprehending peasant woman." (35) Even the narrator's attitude to the rural workers was modified: the 1891 text suggested that such workers were imprudent to marry before they could afford to have children, but in 1912 the narrator concedes that waiting might not make much difference: "for a fieldman's wages being as high at twenty-one as at forty, marriage was early here". (10)

In view of Hardy's revisions, the text used in our discussion of *Tess* is that of the 1912 "Wessex Edition" as reprinted (after changes by Hardy) in 1920. This was the first complete version of the novel, because previous editions had omitted the "Chaseborough Dance" sequence. (10) Unless otherwise indicated, all quotations from *Tess* are from this edition.◆

their sharpness and lead to tragedies of unfulfilment, loss and waste". In *Tess*, class differences "and the nature of class-determined experience" are given especially subtle treatment.

Tess's own position is a complex one. She belongs to the rural poor, but the d'Urberville knights are *her* ancestors, not those of Alec d'Urberville, whose manufacturing family simply annexed the name to give a gloss of respectability to their newly acquired wealth. Tess's family, by contrast, are now called "Durbeyfield", the suffix's shift from "ville" to "field" stressing the rural situation of the declining family. At the same time, the novel repeatedly draws attention to Tess's education: she has been to a "National School" (3) and is more refined than most children of the rural poor. Some readers, notably D.H. Lawrence, have seen her as a kind of natural aristocrat, a refined sensibility trapped in the circumstances of a peasant.

In the presentation of Tess, says the novelist and critic John Bayley, Hardy both evoked and inverted the recurring "Poor Man and the Lady" motif:

> She was an ideal of the peasant girl, the sort of girl who in his earlier novels would have been regarded sympathetically but without personal sentiment, but who has now become the kind of *princesse lointaine* [distant] whom the girl in the grand house once represented. His first

conception of Tess stopped there, but the ingenuity of reverie then provided her with an under-image of the distinction – even the hauteur – possessed by his early aristocratic heroines.

Because of this "under-image" of distinction – this aristocratic ancestry – Tess is haunted by her history. She owes to her paternal d'Urberville heritage certain admirable traits – an air of nobility, a dignified mode of behaviour – but there may be an element of violence, too. The family portraits that she encounters at the start of her blighted honeymoon suggest that some of her female ancestors were capable of "ferocity" and "merciless treachery". (34)

The shadow of her history hangs over her from the start, and the way the narrative is broken into a series of "phases" – The Maiden, Maiden No More, The Rally, etc. – suggests a remorseless progression: what the narrator calls the "almost physical sense of an implacable past" (45) that eventually drives Tess back to Alec and from there to the gallows.

In 1965 the humanist critic Roy Morrell argued in *Thomas Hardy: The Will and the Way* that Tess could have escaped her fate; she was clever enough, and well enough educated, and she had plenty of opportunities. In Morrell's interpretation, she must be seen as a daughter of the shiftless Durbeyfields, and the inheritor of all their lack of resolution:

If "Sir John" Durbeyfield, even with his fatty heart, had the energy to bury the carcase of his horse, he could have dug the ground to grow vegetables for his family; if Tess could bring herself to write the letter of confession [about Alec], she could have made sure Angel received it; if she could endure hardships and humiliations at Flintcomb Ash, she could have risked a snub from Angel's father...

Tess is one of Hardy's gallery of "losers": she has misgivings about Alec d'Urberville and doesn't act on them. "The seduction is not a sudden one; she knows what to expect; but does nothing with the reprieve." Nor does she need to go back to Alec for a second time; she could have escaped Farmer Groby and sought more congenial work, as other girls in his employment did. Always, says Morrell, her tendency is "to drift, to postpone, to leave things to chance".

It is not easy to reconcile this humanist reading of the novel with Hardy's declaration, at the end, about "the President of the Immortals" (59) finishing his sport with Tess. Morrell resorts to claiming that this final paragraph should not be taken literally, though he doesn't really explain why. Philip Larkin found Morrell's reading of the novel bizarre, as if Hardy's moral is that all that is needed to overcome life's difficulties is a little backbone and determination. Larkin writes:

I do not recollect that [Mr Morrell] says anywhere that Hardy is a cheerful writer, but it would be difficult to deduce from his book that he finds him a melancholy one.

Despite Morrell's efforts to see it otherwise, the imagery of the novel emphatically and constantly suggests that Tess is doomed. After the death of Prince, she feels herself "almost a murderess" (4); later, when dairyman Crick is listening to Tess talking about how she day-dreams, his "great knife and fork [are] planted erect on the table like the beginning of a gallows". (18) Early in the novel we are told about the "curious legend" (2) of a white hart killed in a local forest despite the then king Henry III's injunction that it should be spared. Like the white hart, and like the dying pheasants she later puts out of their misery, Tess, too, will be hunted down and destroyed, "harried from place to place at what seems like gradually increasing speed", as John Holloway puts it. She has no escape, her fate being akin to that of the snakes and rats who become victims of the harvest:

Rabbits, hares, snakes, rats, mice, retreated inwards as into a fastness, unaware of the ephemeral nature of their refuge, and of the doom that awaited them later in the day when, their covert shrinking to a more and more horrible narrowness, they were huddled together, friends

and foes, till the last few yards of upright wheat
fell also under the teeth of the unerring reaper,
and they were every one put to death by the sticks
and stones of the harvesters.(14)

There seems little doubt Hardy had Tess in mind
when he wrote this passage. She, too, is trapped:
she is "a bird in a springe" and, at another point,
"a bird caught in a clap-net". When deserted by
Angel, Tess anticipates "falling into some fearful
snare". The complex series of unfortunate events
in the plot resembles a net in which the heroine
is increasingly entangled. In the face of this,
readings like Morell's seem perverse. Tess's own
nature – her mixture of pliability, honesty and
stubbornness – is simply one of the forces that
conspire to destroy her.

How does Hardy use colour in *Tess*?

Hardy is an intensely visual novelist: it is what is most distinctive about his art. Above all, says Tony Tanner in a famous essay, "Colour and Movement in *Tess of the d'Urbervilles*", he makes us "see", and those who complain of the occasional "turgidity of his thoughts" may be overlooking "the incomparable clarity of his eyes". Tanner was a clever and prolific late 20th century critic who has written what are often boldly original essays on 19th century fiction, and he makes as good a case as anyone for Hardy's greatness. He concedes that Hardy is not subtle in the way that Henry James and many subsequent modernist writers are subtle. But for all James's "scrupulous indirectness", Hardy's art "is more truly impersonal". The very crudities of effect which critics so often mock in Hardy gives his work its power, Tanner argues: the schematic characters (in *Tess*), the freakish chances which determine their fate, and the melodramatic incidents, all give to the novel "an anonymity which we more commonly associate with the folk-tale, or the ballads".

As an artist for whom visibility mattered above all else, colour was vitally important to Hardy; in *Tess* one colour catches the eye from the beginning: red, "the colour of blood, which is associated with Tess from first to last":

> It dogs her, disturbs her, destroys her. She is full of it, she spills it, she loses it. Watching Tess's life we begin to see that her destiny is nothing more or less than the colour red.

The red in *Tess* is often set against white. When we first see her, at the May dance, she is wearing a white dress, like all the other girls, but she is the only one with a red ribbon in her hair. "In that simple scene and colour contrast is the embryo of the whole book and all that happens in it." The patterning of red and white is often there in the background, too. At one point Tess sees the "ripe

THE SERIAL VERSIONS

Even before the book appeared, trouble loomed. F. W. Tillotson & Son had agreed to publish a serial version; but, after seeing the proofs of approximately half the novel, they expressed dismay, and, when Hardy declined to censor the material, cancelled the contract. Hardy then offered the manuscript to Edward Arnold at *Murray's Magazine* and Mowbray Morris at *Macmillan's Magazine*. Arnold rejected it, citing "immoral situations". Morris declined it mainly on the grounds of its sexiness – though the term he used was "succulence", of which he found far too much in *Tess*. He also deemed the thought and language sometimes unclear. Later, in the *Quarterly Review,* Morris

hue of the red and dun kine" absorbing the evening sunlight, "which the white-coated animals returned to the eye in rays almost dazzling, even at the distant elevation on which she stood". (16) In Chapter 2 we are told that she is "a mere vessel of emotion untinctured [untinged] by experience". Tess is often seen as a "white shape" (7); on the night of her seduction or rape, for example, she is a "white muslin figure" sleeping on a pile of dead leaves; her "beautiful feminine tissue" (11) is described as "practically blank as snow".

The "tincturing" of Tess by experience starts early, prefigured by the story of the white hart and by that red ribbon which sets her apart from her friends. Then comes the death of Prince, one of the

said that Hardy had told "a coarse and disagreeable story in a coarse and disagreeable manner". Hardy reflected: "If this sort of thing continues, no more novel-writing for me. A man must be a fool to deliberately stand up to be shot at." When the novel was finally serialised, Alec's early relationship with Tess was confirmed, to spare the blushes of magazine readers, by a bogus marriage instigated by Alec and deemed genuine by Tess. Notoriously, in the serial version, Angel does not carry the dairymaids in his arms across the flooded lane's pool; instead, he transports them in a wheelbarrow.

Within 30 years of *Tess*'s first appearance, D. H. Lawrence, in such works as *The Rainbow* and *Women in Love*, was able to depict sexual encounters with a frankness which would have been impossible for Hardy. Hardy, however, had in various ways eroded the barriers of censorship and thus prepared the way for Lawrence.◆

most graphic passages in the novel. Tess, while driving the bee-hives to market, falls asleep and Prince collides with the mail cart in the early morning darkness.

> *The pointed shaft of the cart had entered the breast of the unhappy Prince like a sword, and from the wound his life's blood was spouting in a stream, and falling wit h a hiss into the road.*
>
> *In her despair Tess sprang forward and put her hand upon the hole, with the only result that she became splashed from face to skirt with the crimson drops. Then she stood helplessly looking on. Prince also stood firm and motionless as long as he could; till he suddenly sank down in a heap. (4)*

At its most basic, this incident means that the family is now destitute. It is also the first in a series of images of penetration, culminating in the knife thrust which finally kills Alec. Tanner writes:

> It adumbrates the loss of her virginity, for she, too will be brutally pierced on a darkened road far from home; and once the blood of her innocence has been released, she too, like the stoical Prince, will stay upright as long as she can until, all blood being out, she will sink down suddenly in a heap. Compressed in that one imponderable scene we can see her whole life.

After the mail cart leaves, the darkness begins to lift, and once again we have the image of red against white: the lane "showed all its white features, and Tess showed hers, still whiter" while the "huge pool of blood" in front of her assumes "the iridescence of coagulation". The symbolism of the detail is "naïve and forthright to the point of temerity", writes Dorothy Van Ghent. Van Ghent's stimulating essay on Tess, published 15 years earlier than Tanner's, in her book *The English Novel: Form and Function*, takes a similar view to Tanner's. Like him she is struck by the bold use of symbolism and by the starkness of some of the visual effects. When Tess "put her hand upon the hole" (4) in Prince's chest, the gesture, says Van Ghent, "is as absurdly ineffectual as all her effort will be; the only result is that she becomes splashed with blood – as she will be at the end..."

Following the death of Prince, Tess constantly encounters the colour red – if not blood, then reminders of it. Alec's new house is "rich red" (5), while the building where she is finally executed in Wintoncester is "a large red-brick building". (59) ("Red marks the houses of sex and death," says Tanner.) Alec presses a strawberry to her lips – which resemble "roses filled with snow" (24) – and gathers roses to adorn her hat and bosom; later, the thorn of a rose pricks her skin. Alec, says the narrator, "stood fair to be the blood-red ray in the spectrum of her young life" (5); on the night of her downfall, Tess sees "the red coal of his cigar". (10)

Shortly after leaving Alec for the first time, she encounters a man painting a slogan on a wall (with commas between each word to give added emphasis) – "THY, DAMNATION, SLUMBERETH, NOT". He is using a "tin pot of red paint" and the result is that his "vermilion letters shone forth". (12) Back home, Tess sees sunlight breaking through chinks of the cottage shutters, "throwing stripes like red-hot pokers upon cupboards, chests of drawers, and other furniture within". (14) A reaping machine has ruddy-painted arms, which, in sunlight, seem "dipped in liquid fire". (14) A herd of cows is "red and white". (16) The threshing machine on which Tess is eventually forced to work is bright red. The culmination of this sequence is the "scarlet blot" of blood on the white ceiling after the murder of Alec; it resembles – ironically, in a tale of destructive passion – a "gigantic ace of hearts". (56)

All these images are integral to the novel. Hardy insisted (despite the aggressive sub-title and early Preface) that *Tess* was "an impression, not an argument", and it is this impression, or series of impressions, to which sympathetic critics have responded. There is a dream-like quality to Hardy's novels, one reason why he is sometimes seen as anticipating modernists such as James Joyce. Consider the unforgettable scene in *Far From the*

Madding Crowd in which Sergeant Troy dazzles Bathsheba with his sword-play: it is, of course, implausible, but, as Claire Tomalin notes in her fine biography of the author, it is Hardy the poet whom we here see at work, "conjuring up a perfect metaphor for seduction". *The Return of the Native* is like a sombre version of Shakespeare's *A Midsummer Night's Dream*, with witches instead of fairies, fierce quarrels, rustics who put on a dramatic entertainment, a moonlit love scene and even a young woman who disguises herself as a boy. It, too, is like a dream, or rather a nightmare, and one in which characters and landscape reflect each other.

That Tess, immediately after her defloration, should run into a man painting a harsh Old Testament warning on a wall also seems like something out of a nightmare. But it is part of the mysterious logic of Hardy's world that this should happen, and of the simple, elemental story that he is telling, just as the recurrent use of red is there to reinforce our sense of Tess's destiny. "Life starts in sex and ends in death," says Tanner, "and Hardy constantly shows us how closely allied the two forms of blood-letting are in one basic, unalterable rhythm of existence."

Is Tess raped – or seduced – by Alec?

The early critics of Tess were adamant: she is the author of her own misfortunes. This is the story not of a girl "pure at heart", whatever Hardy tells us, said Mowbray Morris in the *Quarterly Review* of April 1892; it is one of a girl who "rises through seduction to adultery, murder and the gallows". In the immensely popular *Blackwood's Magazine*, the novelist Mrs Oliphant was even more scathing: while Tess's first downfall might not contradict the "defiant blazon of a Pure Woman", her decision to become "the mistress of her seducer" cannot be explained away by "any stress on poverty or misery". Come off it, said Mrs Oliphant. Tess was a skilled labourer, "for whom it is very rare that nothing can be found to do. Here the elaborate and indignant plea for Vice, that is really Virtue, breaks down altogether."

In their emphasis on Tess's personal responsibility, later echoed by humanists such as Roy Morrell, these Victorian critics take it for granted that Tess was seduced and not raped. But the luckless maiden seduced in the 1890s begins to look more like the luckless victim of rape in the permissive 1960s. Tony Tanner's 1968 verdict is unequivocal: Tess is raped. Some modern commentators, like Simon Gatrell, agree; others at the very least hedge their bets. Margaret Drabble's fifth edition of *The Oxford Companion to English Literature* (1984), for example, states: "Tess is cunningly seduced". Ian Gregor thinks the deed was "both a seduction and a rape". (Try that in court, says John Sutherland.) While the novelist and critic David Lodge maintains that Tess is "seduced, not raped", James Gibson, writing in the 1990s, the era of "date rape", talks edgily of Tess's "sexual molestation by Alec"; later, in an introduction to the Everyman edition, Gibson is bolder, deciding she is raped. H.M. Daleski says that "what happened in the Chase is... so ambiguously presented as to invite... mutually contradictory readings", while Kristin Brady finds that "it is in the end impossible to ascertain precisely what happened". Is it? What really happens in the Chase – seduction, "cunning" seduction, violation, "virtual rape" or rape?

John Sutherland makes a careful and detailed analysis in his entertaining book, *Is Heathcliff a Murderer? Puzzles in Nineteenth-Century Literature*. Hardy himself, says Sutherland, was unsure about what Mrs Oliphant called the "naughty chapters", agreeing to drop the Chaseborough sequence and substitute for it a sham marriage between Alec and Tess to satisfy nervous editors for the serial version of *Tess* (see page 18). Even when the sequence was finally restored, however, much remained inscrutable.

The episode begins with a description of the Trantridge peasantry's loose morals and hard drinking during an evening of revelry in nearby Chaseborough. Tess, we are told, likes to go to these Saturday night affairs but doesn't participate in the revelry. On the night in question, she eventually leaves Chaseborough to go to a barn in a nearby "townlet" where her fellow Trantridge cottagers are at a "private jig" (10); she wants their company on the way home, since there has been both a fair and a market at Chaseborough and

THE LAW ON RAPE

Hardy, a Justice of the Peace, was well informed about English law. This defined rape as "the offence of having unlawful and carnal knowledge of a woman by force, and against her will". John Mews's *The Digest of English Case Law* (1898, IV, 1,548-9) goes further, saying: "to constitute rape, it is not necessary that the connection with the woman should be against her will; it is sufficient if it is without her consent". *The Laws of England* (1907-17) adds:

> If the woman is asleep when the connection takes place, she is incapable of consent, and although no violence is used, the prisoner may be convicted of rape, if he knew that she was asleep.

Five judges confirmed that a man who had copulated with a sleeping woman was clearly guilty of rape. It is, however, most unlikely that Tess, a virgin, would have remained asleep throughout Alec's onset: she would surely have woken.◆

there may be drunken men in the country lanes. When Tess arrives at the barn, she finds a surreal scene. Its floor is deep in "scroff",

that is to say, the powdery residuum from the storage of peat and other products, the stirring of which by [the dancers'] turbulent feet created the nebulosity that involved the scene..., [a] floating, fusty débris *of peat and hay... (10)*

This dusty haze later merges with the September mist to enshroud the events that follow in a corresponding moral "nebulosity". The scene has been connected to the influence of French impressionists on Hardy, but at a more basic level, says Sutherland, it alludes to a common belief in country communities: "that flying dust, as it gets trapped in their underwear, has a sexually exciting effect on women dancers. It is part of the folklore of barn-dances in America that unscrupulous young men – intending to induce wantonness in their partners – scatter pepper on the boards before the evening gets under way."

The "scroff" certainly seems to have had an aphrodisiac effect in Chaseborough. Hardy hints at a sexual orgy by means of a series of classical references:

They coughed as they danced, and laughed as they coughed. Of the rushing couples there could barely be discerned more than the high lights – the indistinctness shaping them to satyrs clasping nymphs – a multiplicity of Pans whirling a multiplicity of Syrinxes; Lotis attempting to elude Priapus, and always failing. (10)

As Sutherland notes, these allusions signal 'rape'.* Tess, however, refuses to join the dusty dancers and becomes aware of the "red coal" of a cigar behind her. It is Alec, who offers to take her home. Though exhausted – having been up at five every morning – she declines, not quite trusting him, "perhaps forewarned", as Sutherland puts it, "by the phallic heat of [Alec's] Havana on her neck". But when Car Darch, one of Alec's former mistresses, threatens her with violence, she allows herself, now a maiden in distress, to be carried off by Alec on his horse. Chaseborough is only three miles from Trantridge yet Alec deliberately loses his way and, when Tess falls asleep in the saddle, slips his arm round her.

*Syrinx was a beautiful Arcadian river-nymph who had the misfortune to be pursued by the ugly, goat-like Pan. She fled to her river in terror of being ravished and called loudly to the gods to help her. They heard her and in their mercy turned her into a reed (which is what the name "Syrinx" means). Pan, disappointed, cut off many of the reeds and formed the "Pan-pipes" or the shepherd's flute. Priapus, in Greek mythology, was a minor rustic fertility-god best noted for his large erection (giving rise to the term "priapism"). In Ovid's *Fasti*, the nymph Lotis falls into a drunken slumber at a feast, and Priapus seizes the opportunity to advance upon her. Just before he can embrace her, however, a donkey brays. Lotis awakes and pushes Priapus away; and, so that she can permanently escape him, she is then transformed into the lotus flower.

"This immediately put her on the defensive," we are told, "and with one of those sudden impulses of reprisal to which she was liable she gave him a little push from her". (11) Alec almost tumbles from the horse. It is a significant detail, anticipating the final stabbing of Alec by Tess – another "impulse of reprisal". To Sutherland, this shows Tess to be vigilant and "well capable" of defending herself. Alec admits that he brought her "to this out-of-the-way place". Tess for her part repulses his love-making without, as Sutherland says, "ever distinctly denying that she loves him" and Alec, encouraged by her lack of "frigidity", seeks to encourage her further by saying he has bought her family a new horse to replace Prince. Tess nearly falls sleep again, and Alec, now lost, wraps her in his coat and leaves her in a kind of nest made from newly dropped leaves. He goes to find the road; he returns to find her asleep. He bends down to her,

> till her breath warmed his face, and in a moment his cheek was in contact with hers. She was sleeping soundly, and upon her eyelashes there lingered tears. (11)

The narrator then averts his gaze and provides three paragraphs of lofty moralising.

> But, might some say, where was Tess's guardian angel? where was the providence of her simple

faith? Perhaps, like that other god of whom the ironical Tishbite spoke, he was talking, or he was pursuing, or he was in a journey, or he was sleeping and not to be awaked.

The "ironical Tishbite" is the prophet Elijah, who, according to 1 Kings 18:27, mocked the worshippers of Baal for their idolatry. The narrator thus speculates that the Christian God is no more available to help those who need succour than was Baal for the pagans who were afflicted by drought and famine. (The phrase "that other god", with its appropriate lower case "g", is slyly derogatory of the deity who is usually accorded an upper-case "G".) Hardy then asks rhetorically

RAPE AND SEDUCTION
IN LITERATURE

Famous examples of rape in literature include: Lucretia or Lucrece, commemorated in Shakespeare's narrative poem (and cited in Hardy's novel); Lavinia, daughter of Titus Andronicus; and the eponymous heroine of Samuel Richardson's novel, *Clarissa*. In each case the rapist is punished: by exile, in the case of Tarquin, violator of Lucretia; by death at the hands of Titus for Chiron and Demetrius, violators of Lavinia; and by death in a duel, for Lovelace, violator of Clarissa. But in each case, too, the victim dies. Lucretia kills herself to expunge the "dishonour"; Lavinia is slain by her

why, "upon this beautiful feminine tissue, sensitive as gossamer, and practically blank as snow as yet", there should have been traced "such a coarse pattern as it was doomed to receive". One answer, he suggests, is "retribution":

> *Doubtless some of Tess d'Urberville's mailed ancestors rollicking home from a fray had dealt the same measure even more ruthlessly towards peasant girls of their time.*

Does this image suggest that Alec's deed was an act of rape? The American critic William A. Davis Jr, thinks it does. We are told Tess "had been caught... like a bird in a springe": such a bird has no choice.

---

father; and Clarissa chooses to waste away. The pattern of the double death is maintained in Tess.

Hardy also knew that various 19th-century novels had dealt with the theme of seduction, notably Scott's *The Heart of Mid-Lothian*, Dickens' *David Copperfield*, George Eliot's *Adam Bede*, Mary Gaskell's *Ruth* and Anthony Trollope's *The Vicar of Bullhampton*.

In *Hardy of Wessex*, Carl J. Weber suggests that the victim tended to be "a weakling; she was set in contrast with the heroine who held the centre of the stage". Trollope said: "I could not venture to make this female the heroine of my story." There were exceptions: Ruth's sufferings and redemption are fully portrayed. Unlike Trollope, but following the example of Richardson and Gaskell, Hardy gives fulness, strength and centrality, as well as his sympathy, to the female victim.◆

But, if Alec tries to rape her, why, wonders
Sutherland, doesn't she resist him? A virgin, she
would hardly have slept throughout Alec's
onslaught; the point has already been made that
even while drowsy she is able to fend him off.
"Why does she not protect her imperilled virtue
with one of those timely 'impulses of reprisal'?"

More significantly, when Tess later upbraids
Alec, it is not to accuse him of rape but of having
duped her: "I didn't understand your meaning
until it was too late," she says. (12) Nor, when she
takes her mother to task for not warning her
against men, does she claim she has been raped.
Hardy glosses her thoughts like this:

> She had never wholly cared for [Alec], she did not
> at all care for him now. She had dreaded him,
> winced before him, succumbed to adroit
> advantages he took of her helplessness; then,
> temporarily blinded by his ardent manners, had
> been stirred to confused surrender awhile: had
> suddenly despised and disliked him, and had run
> away. (12)

William Davis thinks the first part of this long
sentence indicates rape, the violation of the
helpless, while the second part, after "then",
almost certainly refers to her later seduction by
Alec while she continues in his employment; the
last part, after the colon, refers to her present

escape from him. John Sutherland, in contrast, thinks the first two thirds of the sentence refer to the episode in the Chase: when Hardy tells us Alec has been "adroit", some cunning caresses with his hands are implied. Sutherland writes:

> [Alec's] "ardent manners" (an odd conjunction – ardour is rarely well-mannered) had "stirred" Tess – erection is hinted at. The verb "stirred" is significant, suggesting as it does physical reciprocation on Tess's part. Did she consent? "Confused surrender" suggests that she did, but that she was blinded at the time by his stimulating foreplay and the power of her own aroused feelings.

Sutherland's conclusion is that Alec is a cad, not a rapist: by Victorian legal lights his action was clearly seduction, with Tess a willing if misguided participant in her own undoing. This view is supported by an earlier episode which anticipates what happens in the Chase. This is the moment when, during an early meeting, Alec persuades Tess to take into her mouth a strawberry – forced and out of season – that she only half resists, parting her lips "in a slight distress" (5) to take it in. As the critic Allan Brick has noted, this seems graphically to reflect the "physical particularities" of Tess's downfall.

The novelist knows everything, as Thackeray reminds us, but Hardy himself said little to cast light on what happened. Few critics nowadays go as far as Tony Tanner did in 1968, asserting that Tess was definitely raped; Penny Boumelha, like a number of modern critics, sees the scene as ambiguous. Hardy himself once told an interviewer, many years after Tess's publication, that she was a victim of "seduction pure and simple". But this novel about "A Pure Woman" underwent many changes. In one early version, Tess is trapped by a bogus marriage ceremony; in another, Alec drugs her before deflowering her. Crucially, in the later text authorised by Hardy, when workmen discuss Tess's baby, one says:

> *"A little more than persuading had to do wi' the coming o't, I reckon. Those were they that heard a sobbing one night last year in The Chase; and it mid ha' gone hard wi' a certain party if folks had come along." (14)*

So the complexities of the novel, and particularly its many variants over the years, leave plenty to divide the critics. Commentators are thus teased by "the opacity factor", which occurs when an important area of a text contains an opacity made all the more conspicuous by the vivid clarities around it. Shakespeare in *Hamlet* and Conrad in *Heart of Darkness* exuberantly exploited this opacity factor: a sure way of soliciting intelligent audiences and generating perennial arguments.

What do Alec and Angel have in common?

Superficially, Alec d'Urberville and Angel Clare could scarcely be more different. Alec is the caddish squire of traditional fiction, the well-to-do man who sees young women as prey to be hunted: he "swaggers and twirls his moustache like the villain in every Victorian melodrama", says A.L. Alvarez. Angel Clare is almost the opposite. Superficially, if Alec is Evil, Angel is Good. By making him a minister's son and giving him his name and his harp – who but Hardy would dare to give a character called Angel a harp? – he creates a figure who stands in almost ridiculously sharp contrast to Alec.

The distinction between the two, crude as it is, is very much to Hardy's purpose. Angel is more complicated than Alec, but his treatment of Tess is chilling and, Hardy implies, more heartless than Alec's. As Dorothy Van Ghent says, "extreme implies extreme, and both Angel and Alec are foundered in egoism, the one in idealistic egoism, the other in sensual egoism, and Angel himself is diabolic enough in his prudery". The truth is that Alec and Angel are not as opposed as they might appear; in a fundamental sense they are quite alike, or at least complementary.

Alec is generally thought the less successful creation of the two. Trevor Johnson calls him "one of the least convincing characters Hardy ever drew". He lacks even "the superficial dash" of Sergeant Troy in *Far from the Madding Crowd*, says Michael Irwin. "Alec comes across as neither physically striking, and therefore conceivably attractive to Tess, nor as innately sensual..." The physical features Hardy chooses to stress – the full lips, the curled moustache, the "bold rolling eye" – are those of a stereotyped lady-killer. His idiom is similarly stagey:

> *"Upon my honour!" cried he, "there was never before such a beautiful thing in Nature or Art as you look, 'Cousin' Tess". (9)*

Alec's later phase of conversion to evangelical Christianity has struck some critics as out of character, a product of Hardy's love of cruelly ironic patterning rather than of likely psychological development. (The same device – a temporary conversion subverted by sexual desire – is used for Arabella in *Jude the Obscure*.) His relapse from piety is accompanied, again, by dialogue befitting stage melodrama:

> *"You temptress, Tess; you dear damned witch of Babylon – I could not resist you as soon as I met you again!" (46)*

Alec also comes close to a melodramatic

Augustus John's 1923 portrait of Hardy

stereotype when, wielding a pitchfork against a
background of fire, he says to Tess: "You are Eve,
and I am the old Other One come to tempt you in
the disguise of an inferior animal." (50) (Tess has
previously imagined Satan wielding a "three-
pronged fork". (14))

Yet those critics who agree with the early
reviewer in *Punch* that Alec is "absurdly

melodramatic", a "stage-scoundrel", or with Simon Gatrell that he is "little more than a cardboard cut-out, two-dimensional rapist and bounder", may forget that sometimes, in real life, individuals (Rasputin and Hitler, for instance) do resemble melodramatic figures, just as, in reality, events occasionally emulate those of melodrama. Besides, Alec does offer to marry Tess, even procuring the licence; he does keep his word about helping the family; and he is fascinated by Tess, valuing her much more highly than his other mistresses (who were relatively uncouth and markedly less beautiful).

So, what of Angel Clare? Michael Irwin finds him as unsatisfactory as Alec, and with even less physical presence:

> How many readers remember that he has a shapely moustache and straw-coloured beard? (17) His mode of speech, pompous and unidiomatic, is if anything less credible and less appealing than Alec's.

Irwin cites his reaction on first becoming aware of Tess at the dance – "What a fresh and virginal daughter of Nature that milkmaid is!" (18) – and is scathing about Angel's notion of affectionate banter:

> *"My Tess has, no doubt, almost as many experiences as that wild convolvulus out there on*

the garden hedge, that opened itself this morning
for the first time." (28)

J.T. Laird also finds the characterisation
of Angel, though interesting, not fully successful.
He suggests that Angel is descended from earlier
"ineffectual" Hardy heroes such as Henry Knight
in *A Pair of Blue Eyes* and Giles Winterbourne in
The Woodlanders. Both these characters, says
Laird, tend to idealise the women they love and
avoid taking "those courses of action which alone
could lead to physical consummation of their
love".

The name "Angel Clare" suggests "bright angel"
(the French *clair* meaning "light" or "bright"), but
one bright angel was Lucifer ("Light-bearer"), who
fell from Heaven to Hell, so the name is possibly
ill-omened; and, as the text emphasizes, it is
certainly ironic, for this Angel – whose harp-
playing is "poor" (19) – is a sceptic in matters of
religion and proves, for all his emancipated ideas,
to be unalterably conventional at heart and an
utter hypocrite in matters of sexual morality.

He is morally divided, even confused.
He regards Tess as a "fresh and virginal daughter
of Nature", a "visionary essence of woman"; but,
though he tries to oppose social snobbery, he is
delighted to find that she can be called "Mistress
Teresa d'Urberville", for then she may more
readily gain acceptance in higher social circles,

after he has made her into "the well-read woman". (30) * He values what he sees as her pure innocence, but, like a new Pygmalion, he seeks to transform her appropriatively (hence Alec's later observation that Tess can "speak so fluently" (45)). Angel is always torn between conflicting impulses. At the beginning he dances with the village girls, unlike his brothers, but then runs after both of them to join in a discussion of "A Counterblast to Agnosticism". (2) Even the clothes he wears at Talbothays, as Michael Irwin notes, suggest a divided personality, a Victorian gentleman imperfectly disguised as a farmer: "Under his linen milking-pinner he wore a dark velveteen jacket, cord breeches and gaiters, and a starched white shirt." (17)

What Hardy shows, according to Rosemary Sumner in *Thomas Hardy: Pscyhological Novelist*, is that Angel's attitude to life is based on "unresolved conflicting views".

> Intellectually, he has rejected his father's dogma, but emotionally he is torn between austerity and sensuousness, rigidity and spontaneity.

This conflict within him may be manageable

*Angel's attitude towards Tess's ancestors is constantly changing, as Dale Kramer shows in his book *The Forms of Tragedy*. He swings between hating "the aristocratic principle of bood" and being very sympathetic to it – depending on his feelings for Tess at any given moment.

before he meets Tess, but once strong feelings become involved it ceases to be abstract and theoretical. On his return to Talbothays after a visit to his parents, his state of mind is more complicated than he thinks it is. Carrying Tess across the flooded lane, he can't decide whether to kiss her or not. He nearly does, then doesn't: "suspension at this point was desirable now". (23)

A little later he acts on impulse to embrace her, but Hardy reminds us that this spontaneous act is in opposition to his normal way of behaving. "Resolutions, reticences, prudences, fears, fell back like a defeated battalion". (24) Even now, though she responds to him with an "ecstatic cry", he doesn't kiss her, instead saying: "Forgive me... I ought to have asked – I did not know what I was doing". When the love between them is eventually acknowledged, Angel still feels "disquieted". (25) Hardy speaks of "the æsthetic, pagan sensuous, Pagan pleasure in natural life and lush womanhood" (25) which Angel had been experiencing. This may seem exaggerated, given that by then they have experienced only one passionate embrace, but in the light of Angel's customary restraint, says Sumner, the feeling of "pagan, sensuous pleasure" is understandable. In contrast to his brothers, Angel has indeed felt what Hardy calls "the great passionate pulse of existence".

Like Alec, however, he neither understands

Tess, nor makes any real attempt to do so. Significantly, neither Alec nor Angel has to work, unlike Tess. "Each represents a deformation of masculinity, one high, one low," says one of Hardy's most sympathetic 20th-century critics, Irving Howe: "they cannot appreciate, cannot even see the richness of life that Tess embodies". Of the two, Alec is preferable, "commonplace vice" being easier to bear than "elevated righteousness". D.H. Lawrence agreed. While Alec at least "seeks with all his power for the source of stimulus in a woman", Angel, as a result "of generations of ultra-Christian training, [has] an inherent aversion to the female."

Penny Boumelha thinks that Alec and Angel both see Tess as a representative of the "nature" of woman, and project on to her their own "various constructions of female sexuality". They seek to make Tess "stand for the whole female sex". For Alec, Tess says what all women say, yet does what all women do:

"I didn't understand your meaning till it was too late."
"That's what every woman says."
"How can you dare to use such words!" she cried... . "My God! I could knock you out of the gig! Did it never strike your mind that what every woman says some women may feel?" (12)

For Angel, on the other hand, Tess represents a more spiritualised, ethereal version of womanhood:

> She was no longer the milkmaid, but a visionary essence of woman – a whole sex condensed into one typical form. He called her Artemis, Demeter, and other fanciful names half teasingly, which she did not like because she did not understand them.
> "Call me Tess," she would say askance; and he did. (20)

The degree to which Alec and Angel are alike is constantly hinted at in the novel. In its patterning, says Boumelha, "the dissolute and amoral Alec and the ascetic and intellectual Angel stand in essentially the same relationship to Tess". In her book, *Thomas Hardy and Women*, Boumelha says the way they are complementary figures is made clear

> not only by Alec's temporary conversion to Evangelicalism and Angel's momentary transformation into a rake with Izz, but also by the similarities between their ways of gaining Tess's acquiescence. It is not only Alec who is associated with gigs and traps that, on occasion, literally run away with Tess; it is during a journey on a wagon driven by Angel that he finally secures

Tess's acceptance of his proposal.

It is worth noting, too, that, just as Alec feeds Tess with berries during her visit to The Slopes, so, during the wagon ride, Angel gives Tess berries that he has pulled from the trees with a whip. Between them, the two men, one by compromising her, the other by rejecting her, drive Tess to her death.

What lies behind Angel's rejection of Tess?

At the heart of the novel, and crucial to an understanding of it, are the passages relating to Angel Clare's "confession" to Tess on the first evening of their marriage, and hers to him. On a social level, Hardy's point is straightforward enough. Angel's confession reveals sexual misconduct which is not just as bad as hers, but worse: he freely chose two days of "dissipation" (34) with a strange woman; Tess, on the other hand, was overcome by a powerful patron when she was vulnerable and exhausted. If anything, her introductory admission to Angel – "'Tis just the same" as yours, she tells him – lets him off lightly.

By his hypocritical disgust at her confession, and by so cruelly leaving Tess to fend for herself hereafter, Angel violates her emotions and

Actress Nastassja Kinski and director Roman Polanski on the set of the film Tess, *1979*

morality more harshly than Alec has violated her body. But Angel's attitude – the attitude which Hardy is attacking – was common enough in those days. The philosopher Arthur Schopenhauer wrote in "The Metaphysics of Love":

> a man is always desiring other women, while a woman always clings to one man; for nature compels her intuitively to take care of the supporter and protector of the future offspring. For this reason, conjugal fidelity is artificial with the man but natural to a woman. Hence, a woman's infidelity, looked at objectively on account of the consequences, and subjectively on account of its unnaturalness, is much more unpardonable than a man's.

The attitude was one embedded in the law: though a man could divorce a woman for adultery, a woman could not divorce her husband for it. Despite his passionate disapproval of this, however, and of the "double standards" involved, Hardy is not unsympathetic in his treatment of Angel, and on a psychological level the story he tells is much more complex than some critics allow. In an interview in August 1892, Hardy described Angel as

> cruel, but not intentionally so. It was the fault of his fastidious temperament. Had he not been a man of great subtlety of mind, he would have followed his brothers into the church. A subtle, poetical man, he preferred that life to the conventional life.

HARDY'S PESSIMISM

"What has Providence done to Mr Hardy that he should rise up in the arable land of Wessex and shake his fist at his Creator?" asked Hardy's friend Edmund Gosse in a review of *Jude the Obscure*. Often, as critics have noted, Hardy seems to plot *against* his characters. When young Jude falls into despair over his Latin and Greek, he wishes "he had never been born". That is a reasonable reaction, says Hardy's biographer, Claire Tomalin, but Hardy continues: "Somebody might have come along that way who

John Bayley, in his elegant analysis of the novel in *An Essay on Hardy*, pays close attention to the two confessions. He notes, first, how it is the news about two of Tess's former colleagues – one of whom has been found drunk while the other has tried to drown herself – which unsettles Tess and makes Angel decide to embark "abruptly" on the mutual "telling of faults". Angel's introductory "It can hardly be more serious, dearest" is a clever touch, says Bayley: in it, Hardy catches "the exact note of self-congratulation in remorse which an adventure with a prostitute might, in that day and age, prompt in recital".

Bayley then makes an obvious though often neglected point: Tess, after her confession, simply *is* a different person to Angel than she was before it – and no amount of moralising about double

would have asked him his trouble, and might have cheered him... But nobody did come, *because nobody does.*" Tomalin puts the last three words into sceptical italics when she quotes them, because, she says, this is not a "true account" of life. "There are times when nobody comes, but there are also times when somebody does come." Hardy himself had been helped to learn by school-teachers and encouraged by architectural masters. A good many people had "come along" for him.

Hardy could have justified some of his pessimism on social grounds, seeing Britain as divided permanently into a nation of rich and poor where women like Tess were being ruthlessly exploited by men like Farmer Groby at

standards "can overcome the actuality of the difference". The passage at the beginning of Chapter 35, after Tess has completed her tale and Angel has begun to become aware of it, is

> the most graphic realisation in Hardy's writings of that commonplace which Dr Johnson referred to: that a man would be as happy in the arms of a chambermaid as of a duchess if it were not for the imagination.

It is the imagination which "determines the direction and force of erotic feeling", and Angel's erotic image of Tess is fixed and overpowering. He discovers that she is not the same person as the one he was infatuated with – and "he is absolutely right". She isn't. The way Angel absorbs the

Flintcomb-Ash. But no one, Tomalin claims, has ever explained where his "black view of life" came from. She herself thinks "something in his constitution made him extraordinarily sensitive to humiliations, griefs and disappointments" – including the suicide of his best friend, Horace Moule – "and that the wounds they inflicted never healed but went on hurting him throughout his life". Perhaps, too, he never got over his loss o f Christian belief, which removed hope. (In "Dover Beach", Matthew Arnold described a world without faith as having "neither joy, nor love, nor light, / Nor certitude, nor peace, nor help for pain".) Whatever the cause, his sense of the world's random cruelty never left him.◆

information is brilliantly shown by Hardy:

> *Clare performed the irrelevant act of stirring the fire; the intelligence had not even yet got to the bottom of him. After stirring the embers he rose to his feet; all the force of her disclosure had imparted itself now. His face had withered. In the strenuousness of his concentration he treadled fitfully on the floor. He could not, by any contrivance, think closely enough; that was the meaning of his vague movement. When he spoke it was in the most inadequate, commonplace voice of the many varied tones she had heard from him. (35)*

What Hardy shows so vividly here is Angel's dawning apprehension of what Tess's revelation means – the "inadequate commonplace voice" suggests what Bayley calls "the plodding of ordinary sequent consciousness"; it also suggests "the weakness in Clare which the reader, but not Tess, is already well aware of..."

The central weakness in Clare is that he is a divided personality. He is "consistently inconsistent throughout", wrote William Watson in *The Academy* in February 1892. (Watson was exceptional among early reviewers in recognizing Angel's complexity.) Some 90 years later, Rosemary Sumner turned to the psychologists Freud and Jung in an effort to explain him. In particular, Sumner explored Clare's personality through the Jungian notion of the "anima".

Jung thought there were masculine and feminine traits in everyone, and gives the name "anima" to "the woman in man". He maintains that men are nearly always unconscious of their anima, and have enormous difficulty recognising it for what it is; what they tend to do is project it on to women to whom they are attracted – with disastrous results, since they are projecting their own picture of womanhood on to someone who is very different. "Since the image is unconscious," says Jung, "it is always unconsciously projected on to the person of the beloved, and it is one of the chief reasons for passionate attraction or aversion."

Something like this occurs in Angel. He is quite explicit in his reasons for rejecting Tess. "You were one person: now you are another... The woman I have been loving is not you." (35) A little later he reflects: "She was another woman than the one who had excited his desire." (36) He has been idealising Tess in very much the way Jung describes: we don't have to accept all Jung's theories, or Freud's, to see that in many respects Hardy often thought along the same lines.

A good illustration of this is the scene in which Angel sleepwalks, with Tess in his arms, then places her in an open grave. Many critics have dismissed the scene as implausible, but Freud would have understood it perfectly. Dreams give us our best access to the unconscious mind, he thought: "the dreamer knows in his unconscious thoughts all that he has forgotten in his conscious ones". This, says Sumner, corresponds to Angel's expression of his love for Tess when he is sleepwalking – the love, repressed in his waking thoughts, re-emerges in the dream – but in his trance-like state he also sees Tess as dead because, even in a dream, he cannot contemplate seeing her as she really is.

Angel's rejection of Tess is undoubtedly related to his idealization of her. "It is in your own mind, what you are angry at, Angel; it is not in me," Tess tells him. (35) When she no longer embodies for him the sense of rustic innocence which attracted him, he begins to despise her, and his earlier slightly patronising attitude – "You are a child to me" (30) – turns into something closer to contempt: "You almost make me say you are an unapprehending peasant woman". (35) Freud referred to "the narcissistic rejection of women by men, which is so mixed up with despising them", when love has displayed "marked sexual over-valuation".

If Angel's love is of this narcissistic, self-regarding kind, his way of dealing with disappointment is, typically, to fall back on his intellect. "He was becoming ill with thinking; eaten out with thinking, withered by thinking..." (36)

Thinking, the narrator of *The Return of the Native* tells us, is "a disease of flesh"; it is a disease also evident in Angel. Hardy frequently emphasizes the "hard logical deposit" in him. He is represented, says Sumner (again using Freudian terms), as "conditioned to repression" not only by his background but also by the means he has used to escape it: an over-reliance on his intellect. His rejection of Tess is ruthless, much worse than Alec's because it is so calculated in its cruelty; but it is psychologically plausible. Whatever weight one might attach to the theories of Jung and Freud, whose abstractions are critically anticipated by Hardy's particularities, Sumner is surely right in seeing Angel as more than the insufferable prig he is often condemned for being. There are weaknesses in the way he is handled, most notably in the later sketchy treatment of his change of mind in Brazil, but he is a subtle, not wholly unsympathetic personality. By creating him as such Hardy gives his story a depth it would otherwise lack.

How convincing a figure is Tess?

Hardy loved his most famous heroine. Asked once which of his novels was his favourite, he replied simply: "*Tess*". Shortly after its first publication he

Tess

~~A Daughter~~ of the D'Urbervilles.

Book First.

~~Her Education~~ The maiden

Chapter I.

On an evening in the latter part of May a middle-aged man was ~~coming~~ walking home ~~ward~~ from Stourcastle ~~market~~ town by a lane which led into the recesses of the neighbouring Vale of Blakemore, or Blackmoor. The pair of legs ~~that carried him~~ were rickety. and there was a bias in his ~~or~~ gait that inclined him to the left of a straight line (somewhat).

He occasionally gave a smart nod, as if in confirmation of ~~the~~ some opinion; though he was not ~~thinking~~ thinking of anything in particular. An empty egg-basket was slung upon his arm, ~~Presently~~ and the nap of his hat was ruffled ~~by~~. Presently he was met by an elderly parson astride on a grey mare, who, as he rode, hummed a wandering tune.

"Good-night," said the ~~countryman~~ pedestrian with the basket.

"Good-night, Sir John," said the parson.

The man with the basket, after another pace or two, halted, & turning round ~~called to the last speaker.~~ called to the last speaker. (well as though I know 'ee by sight)

"Now Sir, begging your pardon, of not knowing your name; we met last market-day on this road about this time, & I said 'Good-night', & you made reply 'Good-night, Sir John', as now."

(and a patch worn away at the brim where he seized it to take it off.)

Opening page of the autograph manuscript

told Sir George Douglas: "I am truly glad that Tess the Woman has won your affections. I, too, lost my heart to her." The losing of his heart is central to the novel: Hardy's passion for his heroine gives it an extraordinary power and fascination; it also makes it, in some ways, unsatisfactory: unlike his previous heroines, Tess is, perhaps, too good to be true.

Hardy establishes her physical attributes with a wealth of detail. She has "a flower-like mouth and large tender eyes" (14); her hair is "earth-coloured" (5); her breath tastes "of the butter and eggs and milk and honey on which she mainly lived" (36); Alec relishes the "succulent" physical "amplitude" and "luxuriance" of this "bouncing girl"; to Angel "that little upward tilt in the middle

THE WORLD ACCORDING
TO HARDY

"[Angel Clare] became wonderfully free from the chronic melancholy which is taking hold of the civilized races with the decline of belief in a beneficent Power." (*Tess*, 18)

"The time seems near, if it has not actually arrived, when the chastened sublimity of a moor, a sea, or a mountain will be all of nature that is absolutely in keeping with the moods of the more thinking among mankind." (*The Return of the Native*, 1/1)

" '[The doctor] says it is the beginning of the coming universal wish not to live.' "
(Jude in *Jude the Obscure*, 6/2)

of her red top lip was distracting, infatuating, maddening" (24); at another point "her arm, from her dabbling in the curds, was cold and damp to his mouth as new-gathered mushrooms". (28) She radiates "the brim-fulness of her nature"; and, after sleep, is as "warm as a sunned cat" (27) – a vividly tactile, hug-evoking simile. All these details proved too much for Mowbray Morris, an early reviewer:

> Poor Tess's sensual qualifications for the part of heroine are paraded over and over again with a persistence like that of a horse-dealer egging on some wavering customer to a deal, or a slave-dealer appraising his wares to some full-blooded pasha.

Happiness can be only "the occasional episode in a general drama of pain". (Elizabeth-Jane's closing thought in *The Mayor of Casterbridge*, 45)

Clym's face reflected "the view of life as a thing to be put up with, replacing that zest for existence which was so intense in early civilizations". (*The Return of the Native*, 3/1)

" '[It] seems such a terribly tragic thing to bring beings into the world – so presumptuous – that I question my right to do it sometimes!" (Sue in *Jude the Obscure*, 5/7)

"[Grace] wondered if there were one world in the universe where the fruit had no worm, and marriage no sorrow." (*The Woodlanders*, 28)

"I never cared for Life: Life cared for me." ("Epitaph") ◆

Tess is proud, modest, generous, loyal, strong, courageous, and capable of an enduring and self-sacrificing love. Her domestic upbringing and her numerous tasks are depicted in tellingly realistic detail. Her courageous suffering in adversity, whether toiling in harsh fields or in coping with the death of her child, is knowledgeably and, on the whole, unsentimentally rendered.

Yet there is also a sense in which she is never quite real. Hardy's previous heroines –like Eustacia Vye in *The Return of the Native*, longing to be desired and always dissatisfied – were viewed with an ironic detachment. Tess, unlike Eustacia, or Bathsheba in *Far from the Madding Crowd*, never uses her sexuality to manipulate men, but if she is less scheming than they are she is also less substantial. Irving Howe finds her "that rare creature in literature: goodness made interesting". To the Hardy scholar J.T. Laird, however, she is "a sentimentalized angelic figure". "Tess herself is almost less a personality than a beautiful portion of nature violated by human selfishness and over-intellectualizing," says Kathleen Rogers. "She is the least flawed of Hardy's protagonists, but also the least human."

To Penny Boumelha, she brings out an "unusually overt maleness" in Hardy's normally genderless narrative voice. The narrator is fascinated by her sexuality and his "erotic fantasies of penetration and engulfment enact a pursuit, violation and persecution of Tess in parallel with those she suffers at the hands of her two lovers". Time and again it is as if the narrator seeks to enter Tess:

> through her eyes – "[Angel's eyes] plumbed the deepness of the ever-varying pupils, with their radiating fibrils of blue, and black, and grey, and violet"(27); through her mouth – "he saw the red interior of her mouth as if it had been a snake's" (27); and through her flesh – "as the day wears on its feminine smoothness becomes scarified by the stubble, and bleeds". (14)

The phallic imagery of pricking, piercing and penetration, says Boumelha, serves not only to create an image-chain, linking Tess's experiences from the death of Prince to her final penetrative act of retaliation, but also to satisfy the narrator's fascination with the interiority of her sexuality.

In his book *Sex and Death in the Victorian Novel*, the American critic James Kincaid goes further, believing Tess's "being" is "never more than the formulations of others and herself". She "takes on any shape for those she meets, but it is a conveniently empty shape, ready to be filled in and then longed for". The novel's "most disgusting insistence", says Kincaid, is that we (and by "we" he means principally men) all "formulate others" in the same way. Before Tess is deflowered in the Chase, she is what the narrator calls "a pale nebulousness at [Alec's] feet"; when Angel first sees her (in Chapter 2), she is a "white shape", ominously "so soft in her thin white gown". Tess herself wonders whether she has any integral being, fearing that she is just a part of a historical pattern and that if she reads enough she will discover "in some old book somebody just like me". (19) To others, she is only a generic image, "a fine and picturesque country girl and no more" (2); to most people "only a passing thought" (14); no more than "a transient impression, half forgotten". (5) We are all of us, says Kincaid – Alec, Angel, the narrator, the readers – caught up in what he (Kincaid) sees as the sadistic eroticism of the story. Men, alleges this male critic, don't want women who have real "being"; they "are only too satisfied with the 'white shape'". *Tess of the d'Urbervilles* is like "a titillating snuff movie we run in our own minds".

That is a bizarrely extreme view, though Kincaid is not alone in seeing Tess as insubstantial and in discerning an element of complicity between Hardy and his male characters. Philip Larkin, while finding the narrative of the novel "spotted with absurdity" – "Alec's conversion, Angel's 'eight-and-forty hours' dissipation with a stranger', Tess's proclaimed sexual ignorance" –

didn't think this mattered. On re-reading the book, however, Larkin found himself

> more conscious than I was... of an undercurrent
> of sensual cruelty in the writing – this seems an
> extraordinary thing to say of Hardy, but for all his
> gentleness he had a strong awareness of, and
> even relish for, both the macabre and the cruel...

Perhaps he did, but if Hardy's treatment of Tess has been seen as sensually cruel it has also been seen as fiercely protective. At crucial points in the narrative our access to her consciousness is simply withdrawn; at every moment of crisis, she is either asleep or in a reverie: at Prince's death, at the time of her seduction, during the sleep-walking scene, on Angel's return to find her at the Herons, and when the police find her at Stonehenge.

This withdrawal of access to Tess adds to the impression of her as a "specifically indeterminate" being, says John Bayley. He argues that Hardy was so jealously protective of his heroine that he edited out her deflowering by Alec and a good deal more besides. Of course convention stopped him "at the bedroom door", as it did in all the novels, but with Arabella in *Jude the Obscure* and Bathsheba in *Far from the Madding Crowd* we can imagine what happens beyond it: "all is made quite clear". The same is not true of Tess. Hardy's feeling about his heroine is one of such possessive intensity that he

TEN FACTS ABOUT
TESS OF THE D'URBERVILLES

1.

Tess was first published it in serial form in *The Graphic* (London) in 1890, but only after a number of scenes had been censored or toned down.

2.

Tess has been filmed numerous times for cinemas and television. There were two silent movies (1913 and 1924). Roman Polanski's version appeared in 1979, and Michael Winterbottom's adaptation set in India, *Trishna*, was released in 2011. A BBC adaptation by David Nicholls in 2008 featured Gemma Arterton as Tess.

3.

Art Garfunkel named his first post-Simon & Garfunkel solo album "Angel Clare" after the character of the same name.

4.

Hardy's own name appears in the novel when Dairyman Crick explains Angel's opinions on old families. Crick talks of a number of once potent family names which then lost their significance. Among the families he refers to are the Hardys.

5.

Hardy himself chose Gertrude Bugler, a Dorchester girl, to play Tess in his own theatrical adaptation of the novel in 1924, but, after successfully performing the role in Dorchester, she was prevented from performing it in London by Hardy's wife, Florence, who was jealous. Hardy had said that young Gertrude was the true incarnation of the Tess he had imagined. The novel has frequently been adapted for the stage and a 2007 version was a rock opera entitled *Tess, The New Musical*.

6.

In 1906 an Italian operatic version written by Frédéric d'Erlanger was first performed in Naples. When the opera came to London in 1909, Hardy himself attended the première.

7.

Theresa, from which Tess's name derives, recalls St. Teresa of Avila (1515-1582), a Spanish Carmelite nun and Roman Catholic saint. St Teresa claimed to have experienced periods of religious ecstasy, including the appearance of Christ himself to her, as famously sculpted by Bernini in the Basilica of Santa Maria della Vittoria in Rome.

8.

In spite of the novel's success, it was his second last. Highly sensitive to criticism, he was wounded by harsh early reviews.

9.

Tess didn't start out as Tess. Hardy often changed names when he was writing, and he tried out Love, Cis and Sue, using Woodrow as a surname, narrowing the name down to Rose-Mary Troublefield or Tess Woodrow before finally settling on Tess Durbeyfield.

Tess & Angel Clare in the cattle field; "He jumped up from his seat & went quickly towards the desire of his eyes." 1891 illustration by Joseph Syddall. This appeared alonside the serialisation of Tess *in the 1891 London* Graphic.

10.

Hardy, whose mother's ambition was to become a cook in a gentleman's club, joined two: the Savile, then the Athenaeum. He was an assiduous party-goer, took many holidays, indulged in flirtations and once took his brother to the Moulin Rouge in Paris to see the can-can performed. But, says Claire Tomalin, he always kept a "closed and barred door between the polite and quietly spoken" London socialite and the "raging, wounded inner self who chastised the values of the world he inhabited".

could not have described her either living with Alec, or married in the ordinary sense to Clare. Her life with Alec at "The Herons" is blocked off, a nameless activity in which her physical body is no longer herself, and her marriage can only be consummated in a doomed idyll, out of the world and with no future. Hardy's possessiveness can let her be seduced, and hanged. But though he insists on the passion of her sexuality, as in the embrace she gives Angel in the milk-cart to show how much she loves him, it is protested too much to carry conviction.

It is this, perhaps, which Henry James had in mind when he called the sexuality of the novel a fraud. Most of Hardy's heroines are portrayed with a kind of effortless impassivity; he can view them with intentness and detachment. He found this

WESSEX

"Wessex", meaning "the realm of the Western Saxons", was the ancient name of a large part of south-to-south-west England in the days of the Anglo-Saxons. The name was revived by William Barnes's *Poems of Rural Life* (1868), Hardy (first in *Far from the Madding Crowd*, 1874) and George Eliot (notably in *Daniel Deronda*, 1876). This was the geographical area that Hardy knew intimately, and in his novels he increasingly sought to offer a consistent portrayal of Wessex. A map accompanied editions of his works, and he co-operated

impossible with Tess: there was too much of himself in her. Hardy believed that women were truly sensitive in a way that men could not be – and by creating a girl who was part Durbeyfield, part d'Urberville, part peasant, part aristocrat, he found a way of combining his own consciousness with that of a fictional Wessex heroine.

In a sense then, as Bayley puts it, she is an "apotheosis of having it both ways". She may be an attempt to encapsulate the old adage that "the Colonel's Lady an' Judy O'Grady are sisters under their skins" – an idea in which Hardy strongly believed – but she is also strangely indistinct. Because Hardy is so involved with her, "he can't hold her steadily either before himself or before us".

Perhaps the 19th-century heroine with whom Tess has most in common is Madame Bovary. On

---

with those readers who liked to detect correspondences between fictional names and real locations. In *Tess*, for instance, "Sandbourne" corresponds in location and appearance to Bournemouth, and "Wintoncester" to Winchester.

George Eliot had anticipated Hardy in the full use of rustic figures, even to the extent of seeking vindication in Dutch realist paintings. Her discussion of "these faithful pictures of a monotonous homely existence" in *Adam Bede*, Chap. 17, perhaps suggested the sub-title of Hardy's *Under the Greenwood Tree*, "A Rural Painting of the Dutch School".

Nevertheless, in a range of works and particularly in *Tess*, Hardy brought a greater mastery of rural idioms, a more intimate

the surface, the "pure woman" and the provincial doctor's wife who has a string of scandalous, adulterous affairs could scarcely be more different. Yet in one crucial respect they are similar: both fascinated their creators to such an extent that it made objective portrayal of them very difficult. Flaubert – who believed that life only acquires meaning in art – came to feel so close to his heroine that, after describing how she poisoned herself, he was himself physically sick. Hardy's feelings for Tess were of similar intensity. Supposedly, both Tess and Madame Bovary are shaped by their societies; arguably, what really matters about both of them is their isolation. Bayley writes:

> They are not a part of the worlds they have to live in. Both exist to embody, as they superlatively do,

knowledge of local customs and folklore, and a keener sensitivity to the relationship between the seasons, the immediate action and the long traditions (increasingly being eroded) of the countryside.

Salty vernacular dialogue, humour (sometimes condescending) in the depiction of the rustics, realistic detail, and a subtly nostalgic treatment of pastoral communities in the heart of the English countryside: all these combined to make, for reviewers and the general reader, one of the most attractive features of Hardy's writing. Romanticism, with its high valuation of country-dwellers and the rural, was potent in the Victorian period and remained so even into the 21st century.◆

their creators' sense that consciousness cannot be at home in the conditions of existence.

Neither Tess nor Emma Bovary may be aware of "the gulf that separates them from those who feel at home in life", but there is a gulf: Flaubert seems to experience what Emma experiences; the same is true of Hardy with Tess. They created their heroines, in Bayley's view, "both to disown the world, and to rejoin it by being at one" with their victims, the heroines.

In Hardy's early novels, the characters seem entirely independent of him; this is not true of Tess, or of Jude in *Jude the Obscure*. In *Tess*, Hardy's identification with his heroine gives the novel an extraordinary power but also makes it more uneven and, at times, less credible. His rendering of Tess's thoughts and speech, for example, is not always convincing. As the novelist and critic David Lodge has noted, this is particularly evident when Hardy uses free indirect speech to convey Tess's thinking. Free indirect speech or tacitly-reported discourse (lacking quotation-marks, usually in the past tense, and often without such guidance as "she thought that" or "he said that") requires the novelist to be particularly faithful to the linguistic quality of his character's consciousness, but in Hardy's rendering, Tess's consciousness often seems too sophisticated. Here is an example:

Was once lost always lost really true of chastity?
she would ask herself. She might prove it false if
she could veil bygones. The recuperative power
which pervaded organic nature was surely not
denied to maidenhood alone. (15)

The structure of the last sentence suggests
Hardy is telling us what Tess thought – but the
vocabulary is surely his, not hers.* And though we
are told that Tess "spoke two languages: the dialect
at home, more or less; ordinary English abroad and
to persons of quality" (3), Tess's change of tone
from moment to moment is not always convincing.
A striking instance of this comes after the death of
the baby Sorrow, when Tess asks the parson to give
him a Christian burial, and he baulks at this, calling
it another matter. Tess then asks imperiously:
"another matter – why?". These are the tones of the
aristocrat; immediately afterwards, as John Bayley
notes, we have an "acoustic return to the note of the
haggler's daughter when [Tess] bursts out with 'I'll
never come to your church no more'". (14) More
generally, Hardy's dwelling on Tess's religious
impulses and beliefs is curiously unconvincing;
Hardy demonstrates them as conscientiously as he
can, but, for all his efforts, our impression as readers

---

*The same is true when Tess thinks of the past and how, "whatever
its consequences, time would close over them; they would all in a
few years be as if they had never been, and she herself grassed
down and forgotten". The "grassed down" is pure Hardy.

is that Tess's views about religion are his own.

Much more convincing is her comparison of the stars to apples on a tree, made to little Abraham, her brother, just before Prince has his fatal accident.

> "Which do we live on – a splendid one or a blighted one?
>
> "A blighted one."
>
> " 'Tis very unlucky that we didn't pitch on a sound one, when there were so many more of 'em!"
>
> "Yes."
>
> "Is it like that really, Tess?" said Abraham, turning to her much impressed, on reconsideration of this rare information. (4)

This passage has great power; the way Tess talks is quite credible, though the thoughts she is expressing are clearly her creator's. "Tess gets up and lives because Hardy puts his words into her mouth," says Bayley. And he does so in words she can be imagined as speaking. It is in passages like this that she seems most part of his consciousness. They remind us that, for all the novel's discontinuities and inconsistencies in point of view and tone, its heroine is a truly visionary figure.

How coherent is Hardy's view of nature?

Tess is persistently associated with nature. She is a "daughter of the soil"; she is like a "plant" and a "sapling"; the dew falls on her as naturally as on the grass; on occasions she seems an anonymous, timeless figure, as emphasized here by the use of the present tense: "Thus Tess walks on; a figure which is part of the landscape, a fieldswoman pure and simple, in winter guise..."

In Phase the Third, "The Rally", her "rally" of spirits is associated with summer and particularly with the dairy-farm of Talbothays in "the Valley of the Great Dairies". In contrast to Blackmoor Vale, which she knows well, the new valley has larger fields, different streams: for the Froom waters are not slow and turbid, but "clear as the pure River of Life shown to the Evangelist, rapid as the shadow of a cloud, with pebbly shallows that prattled to the sky all day long. There the water-flower was the lily; the crow-foot here." (John the Evangelist, according to the Book of Revelation, 21:1 and 22:1, saw "a new heaven and a new earth", including "a pure river of water of life".) Tess's spirits therefore lift: "Her hopes mingled with the sunshine in an ideal photosphere which surrounded her as she bounded along against the soft south wind. She heard a pleasant voice in every breeze, and in every bird's note seemed to lurk a joy". (16) That "photosphere" combines external radiance with internal: her resurgent quest for pleasure harmonises with the delightful day and setting. The narrator sensuously evokes "the oozing fatness and warm ferments" (24) of the fertile valley where the cows have "large veined udders" (16) hanging "ponderous as sandbags", their milk already oozing from the teats.

It is here that the attraction between Tess and Angel develops: they "unconsciously studied each other". (20) On a June evening, she is drawn by his harp-strumming:

The outskirt of the garden in which Tess found herself had been left uncultivated for some years, and was now damp and rank with juicy grass which sent up mists of pollen at a touch; and with tall blooming weeds emitting offensive smells – weeds whose red and yellow and purple hues formed a polychrome as dazzling as that of cultivated flowers. She went stealthily as a cat through this profusion of growth, gathering cuckoo-spittle on her skirts, cracking snails that were underfoot, staining her hands with thistle-milk and slug-slime, and rubbing off upon her naked arms sticky blights which, though snow-white on the apple-tree trunks, made madder stains on her skin; thus she drew quite near to Clare, still unobserved of him.

Tess was conscious of neither time nor space. The exaltation which she had described as being producible at will by gazing at a star, came now without any determination of hers; she undulated upon the thin notes of the second-hand harp, and their harmonies passed like breezes through her, bringing tears into her eyes. The floating pollen seemed to be his notes made visible, and the dampness of the garden the weeping of the garden's sensibility. Though near nightfall, the rank-smelling weed-flowers glowed as if they would not close for intentness, and the waves of colour mixed with the waves of sound. (19)

In this opulently sensuous passage, the

THE LANGUAGE IN *TESS*

Hardy delighted in etymologies, dialects and contrasting conventions of language. He contributed to the developing *Oxford English Dictionary* a range of words, some of them dialectal, others being his own new coinages (e.g. "unforefending", "disillusive" and "impercipient").

From the outset, *Tess*'s vocabulary caused problems, particularly the more scholarly terms (such as those coinages): they gave that parody-inviting distinctiveness to Hardy's prose. Early critics and many later ones objected to such diction. Mowbray Morris in the *Quarterly Review* grumbled that Hardy had, like the pedants in *Love's Labour's*

appropriately rich vocabulary ranges from the down-to-earth ("cuckoo-spittle") to the classically Hellenic ("polychrome") and to the technical ("madder", an artist's term for a plant-derived red colouring). Although the general context is an idyllic phase in Tess's life, Hardy here defies sentimental pastoral notions by stressing that this part of the farm is a profuse wilderness of smelly staining weeds. It has its own richness, lushness and energetic amplitude; but, as Tess proceeds, she is repeatedly smeared and stained. (We may recall the "coarse pattern" traced on her by Alec.) She is apparently unaware of the marks, being entranced by the musical sounds; but Hardy arranges an ironic discrepancy between her

---

Lost, "been at a great feast of languages and... stolen the scraps"; William Watson in the *Academy* deplored the "over-academic phraseology".

Sometimes the implication was a snobbish one: the critics felt that Hardy should stay within a vocabulary appropriate to the rendering of "Wessex" and should not sound like a university professor. Sometimes the objection derived from a combination of linguistic ignorance and sheer sloth. Hardy, who never went to university, was a skilled autodidact, and his eloquence reproaches readers who are not prepared to construe some of the terms or simply consult a dictionary. Arguably, the objection stems mainly from readers too myopic to appreciate Hardy's great linguistic project, which was to expand his grasp on the world and its tensions by using an unusually extended vocabulary. In doing so, he was testing the relative utility of different language-conventions, and was showing

exalted state and the physical staining by nature.

Again, he suggests that humans are living paradoxes, their transcendent yearnings being snared by their all-too-physical bodies. Though each detail is realistic enough, the profusion of sliminesses – not only "cuckoo-spittle" but also "thistle-milk", "slug-slime", "sticky blights" and the implied goo from the crushed snails – is so great as to give the first paragraph an expressionistic or almost hallucinatory quality. (Hardy surpasses the similar descriptions in Emile Zola's *La Faute*.)

The second quoted paragraph shows Tess's emotional and sensuous nature. She is not so much hearing the music as blending with it: "she

that different facets of humanity are revealed by different modes of speech. Repeatedly, the language of the learnèd is brought into juxtaposition with the language of the rural workers; classical derivations (Latinate and Hellenic) rub against Anglo-Saxon; and the interaction is mutually critical and mutually enhancive. (Tess speaks two dialects: rural working-class and educated middle-class.)

There is also, obviously, an æsthetic and sensuous element. Hardy rejoiced in rich, strange and diverse sound-patternings; he relished the ways in which "sumple", "blooth", "glane" and "clipped and colled" contrasted orally and aurally with "dolorifuge", "noctambulist", "pachydermatous" and "photosphere"; and, if we value subtle sensuality, so should we. (The words mean "supple", "blossom", "sneer", "embraced and kissed", "solace", "night-walker", "thick-skinned and "sphere of undulated upon the thin notes"; "their harmonies passed like breezes through her"; and it seems to her that the garden too is blending in entrancement, as though seeking synæsthesia, a sensuous confusion: pollen seems to be "notes made visible", and "the waves of colour mixed with the waves of sound". We learn of her sensibility, her intense responsiveness; we seem to inhabit her senses and emotions. She moves through the undergrowth "as stealthily as a cat". In this second paragraph, says Dale Kramer in *Thomas Hardy: The Forms of Tragedy*, "is a fully articulated evocation of a sensitivity too extreme to survive the shocks of a powerful order of material Nature and the grossness of the social world. And thus, the

radiance" – often tamer terms: notice the neutering.)

In *Tess*, our appraisal of the characters is strongly influenced by their vocabularies. When Tess's confession shocks Angel, her simple phrasing poignantly evokes the Lord's Prayer ("Forgive us our trespasses, as we forgive them that trespass against us") as she says: "Forgive me, as you are forgiven"; but that poignant plea meets a bitter response from him:

"O Tess, forgiveness does not apply to the case! You were one person; now you are another. My God – how can forgiveness meet such a grotesque – prestidigitation as that!" (35)

The hypocrisy of his response is stressed by the "My God" from a sceptic; and his cruelty is intensified by that phrase "grotesque – prestidigitation", which emphasises the difference in class and culture between himself and his bride. The polysyllabic phrase is a verbal slap in her face.◆

entire basis for tragedy is condensed into, and expressed through, this one paragraph and its context."

To Dorothy Van Ghent, the passage shows Tess as a victim and anticipates what will happen to her.

> The weeds, circumstantial as they are, have an astonishingly cunning and bold metaphorical function. They grow at Talbothays, in that healing and procreative idyll of milk and mist and passive biology, and they too are bountiful with life, but they stain and slime and blight; and it is in this part of Paradise (an "outskirt of the garden" – there are even apple trees here) that the minister's son is hidden, who, in his conceited impotence, will violate Tess more nastily than her sensual seducer...

David Lodge sees the passage, more simply, as showing how much Tess is a part of the natural world. The garden is an image of the "unconstrained nature" which Angel Clare thinks he wants in a mate. It "seemed natural enough to him... to choose a mate from unconstrained Nature and not from the abodes of Art". (27) Yet Angel does not really want this at all, says Lodge: he is constantly talking to her about the pastoral life in ancient Greece and calling her by classical names, "thus demonstrating that

Opposite: map of Thomas Hardy's Wessex

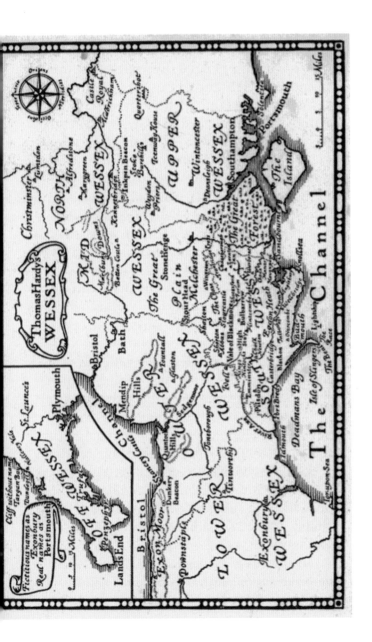

he is not really prepared to accept a mate from unconstrained Nature".

A number of critics believe Hardy's view of nature in *Tess* is divided. Ian Gregor argues that there is a contradiction between a "Rousseauistic view of Nature" as essentially life-giving, healthy, opposed to the inhibiting, destructive forces of society and convention which alone can generate human misery, and the "deterministic [view] which Hardy runs alongside it" in which the world is as a "blighted star". David Lodge says that a whole network of imagery encourages us to think of Tess as "essentially 'in touch' with nature", while it is equally made clear that Nature is wholly indifferent to her and her fate (as when she is seen, on her way to Talbothays, as "like a fly on a billiard table of indefinite length, and of no more consequence to her surroundings than that fly" (16)). John Bayley says that if the pregnant Tess, stealing out in the evening among the rabbits and birds, really felt her state to be as natural as theirs, she would not be the "pure woman" Hardy seeks to present. Nature, after all, is cruel: look at Car Darch, who threatens Tess at Chaseborough, or Arabella in *Jude the Obscure*: both have the simple instincts of nature, "and are as insensitive and as callous", alleges Bayley.

Too much can be made of this. There is an ambivalence in Hardy's vision of the natural world, but it is perfectly plausible that Tess should feel a

part of nature *and* be a victim of it – Hardy shows
her to be both. She feels trapped by her body, by
what the narrator calls her "exceptional physical
nature" (36) and, as a result, the inevitability of an
erotic response from men; she attracts Alec and is
attracted to him, although she wishes she weren't,
and feels guilty because of the reaction she arouses
in others.

> *And there was revived in her the wretched*
> *sentiment which had often come to her before,*
> *that in inhabiting the fleshly tabernacle with*
> *which nature had endowed her she was somehow*
> *doing wrong.(45)*

There are significant parallels between the scene
in the garden where she listens to Angel playing
the harp and the scene where she is overcome in
the Chase: the summer evening "atmosphere", the
music, the references to mist, to slime and to tears
are among the links between the two passages, and
they reinforce the notion that she is doomed.

The idea of the tragic potential of nature and
sexuality is central to the novel, and as much a part
of it as the simple feminist point about society's
double standards. It is there in the suggestions of
an impersonal biological process at Talbothays –
the "stir of germination" (15), the "rush of juices",
the "hiss of fertilization" (24), the "broody hens",
the "farrowing pigs" (29) – and it is there in the

torments suffered by Tess's fellow dairy workers, writhing from the "hopeless passion" thrust on them by "cruel Nature's law", a passion "which they had neither expected nor desired... The differences which distinguished them as individuals were abstracted by this passion, and each was but a portion of one organism called sex." (23)

Nothing society can do will change this. If Tess is damned, and damns herself, by man-made laws which are arbitrary and cruel, she is damned by nature, too. Nature may make a mockery of social laws, as Hardy suggests it does – "The fetish of chastity is a ludicrous aberration in a world which teems and spills with such promiscuous and far-flung fertility," says Tony Tanner – but it is not just society which turns on Tess; nature turns on her too. We "register something approaching a sadism of both the man-made and the natural directed against her": the cold negating metal inside Angel is also to be found in the "steely stars" (50); the pangs of guilt which lacerate her are matched by the "glass splinters" (43) of rain which assail her at Flintcomb-Ash. The sun is a curse as well as a blessing.

When we first see Tess dancing with her friends they are "warmed without by the sun" and also nourished by it – "each of them had a private little sun for her soul to bask in" .(2) At Talbothays, rays from the sunrise "drew forth the buds and stretched them into stalks". (20) Tess meets Angel in the sunless fog before dawn, when she appears as a "visionary essence of woman"; then the sun rises and "her teeth, lips and eyes scintillated in the sunbeams, and she was again the dazzlingly fair dairymaid only..." * But after dairyman Crick tells his story of the seduction of a young girl, she is overcome by sadness and "the evening sun was now ugly to her, like a great inflamed wound in the sky". (21) After her marriage, "at half-past six the sun settles down upon the levels, with the aspect of a great forge in the heavens". (28) Once again the sun is seen as a crushing force, and on this first evening of what should be her honeymoon it settles on her directly, in a sinister way:

> The sun was so low on that short last afternoon of the year that it shone in through a small opening and formed a golden staff which stretched across to her skirt, where it made a spot like a paint-mark set upon her. (34)

The sun gives life but also destroys it. A "shaft of dazzling sunlight" (57) falls on the furniture in the

*J.B. Bullen, in *The Expressive Eye: Fiction and Perception in the Work of Thomas Hardy*, also stresses the major role played by the sun in *Tess*. When Angel and Tess come together at dawn, Bullen says, Hardy "carefully defines the exact quality of light, pointing out that "The grey half-tones of daybreak are not the grey half-tones of the day's close, though the degree of their shade may be the same". In writing *Tess*, says Bullen, Hardy drew on his intimate knowledge of the works of J.M.W. Turner, a painter famous for depicting the effect of light on landscape.

room where she spends her last night, and at
Stonehenge she questions Angel:

> *"Did they sacrifice to God here?" asked she.*
> *"No," said he.*
> *"Who to?"*
> *"I believe to the sun." (58)*

Nature and society, between them, converge on Tess;
she is a victim of both society's conventional
restrictions and nature's blind biological purposes.
The sun rises on her at Stonehenge just as it had
risen on her when she first embraced Angel. Though
herself a fertile source of life, she has come to feel
that "birth itself was a degrading personal
compulsion, whose gratuitousness nothing in the
result seemed to justify". (51)

Caricature of Mr T. Hardy by Leslie Ward, published in
Vanity Fair *in 1892 in a series of 'Men of the Day'*

How big a role does the earth itself play in *Tess*?

In *Tess*, more than any of Hardy's novels, the earth itself plays an important dramatic role. Egdon Heath, in *The Return of the Native*, is obviously important as a setting for the tragic events that occur, but while, as Dorothy Van Ghent says, it may be a metaphor for "the loneliness of human motive" and "the inertia of unconscious life", it is, arguably, not dramatically necessary. Nor are the Roman ruins in *The Mayor of Casterbridge*, though they reflect the futility of human effort and show how everything, in the end, turns to dust. The same idea is present in *Tess*: time has destroyed the d'Urbervilles, and the endless rubbing of cows' flanks is wearing away the walls of the dairy.

But in *Tess*, says Van Ghent, "the earth is primarily not a metaphor but a real thing that one has to move on in order to get anywhere or do anything". Tess has to trudge miles during the novel and weariness contributes heavily to her fate. It is weariness that leads to the accident with the mail cart, and to her defloration: she is exhausted yet has to get from Chaseborough to Trantridge; it is her fatigue which gives Alec his opportunity. After the collapse of her marriage, she is forced to spend brutal months making desolate journeys on foot to seek dairy work and field work. The "insidiously demoralizing" effect of these journeys, says Van

Ghent – made vivid by Tess's plodding trip over the chalk uplands to Flintcomb-Ash – is, again, "an effect of the irreducible thereness of the territory she has to cover". Then comes the grimness of her soul-wearying, ineffectual trip from the farm to Emminster to see Clare's parents, who have no foreknowledge of her coming and are not at home when she gets there. Finally, says Van Ghent,

> with the uprooting and migration of the Durbeyfield family on Old Lady Day, the simple fatality of the earth as earth, in its measurelessness and anonymousness, with people having to move over it with no place to go, is decisive in the final event of Tess's tragedy – her return to Alec, for Alec provides at least a place to go.

Walking, travelling and movement of all kinds are central preoccupations of the novel. The book opens with a man staggering down a road; Phase the Second opens with Tess herself stumbling along with a heavy basket, occasionally stopping to rest "in a mechanical way by some gate or post" (12); Phase the Third sees Tess on the move again: "she left home for the second time". (16) This time she starts in a vehicle, but soon gets out and walks. "Always Tess has to move," says Tanner, "and always Hardy makes sure that we see her." At the end of her wasted journey to see Angel's parents, she loses her walking boots – a reminder that the walking gets harder and harder for her.* "Her journey back was rather a meander than a march. It had no sprightliness, no purpose; only a tendency". (44)

Perhaps the essence of Tess's story is shown in the picture we are given of her running after Angel, having murdered Alec. Angel turns round:

> *The tape-like surface of the road diminished in his rear as far as he could see, and as he gazed a moving spot intruded on the white vacuity of its perspective. (57)*

The scene has been anticipated when Tess is working at Flintcomb-Ash, and is seen, in the same way, as a moving spot on a "white vacuity":

> *the whole field was in colour a desolate drab; it was a complexion without features, as if a face, from chin to brow, should be only an expanse of skin. The sky wore, in another colour, the same likeness; a white vacuity of countenance with the lineaments gone. So these two upper and nether visages confronted each other all day long... without anything standing between them but the two girls crawling over the surface... like flies. (43)*

Here, says Tanner, Tess is a "visible paradigm" of the

---

*In a further irony, Mercy Chant, a former rival for Angel's hand, appropriates the boots.

terms in which Hardy saw human life – a spot of "featured animation moving painfully across a vast featureless repose". Eventually, at the place of sacrifice at Stonehenge, she will give up the struggle and lie down. Her instinct is for placidity, yet constantly she is forced to move, not just on foot but also on men's machines: driving her father's bee-hives to market; driven recklessly by Alec in his dog-cart – though "the least irregularity of motion

ALWAYS ON THE MOVE

The reader gets to know Wessex well because characters are frequently traversing its terrain, often on foot, sometimes on horse-back or in a horse-drawn cart or gig. Tess herself covers 30 miles in one walk – to Angel's home and back. When her father dies, the lease of his cottage expires; and, following a quarrel over the "harbouring" of Tess there, the family must migrate in a heavily-laden cart. It thus adds to the traffic on roads used not only by the annual Candlemas treks of workers seeking new contracts but also by the families who, no longer being needed in their villages, are heading for the towns. If Tess's journeys sometimes resemble a *via crucis* ("Road of the Cross", the ordeal of Jesus) or an ironic contrast to Bunyan's *The Pilgrim's Progress* (in which Christian is eventually rewarded for his ordeals), the novel's general emphasis on travelling generates a theme of deracination: a widespread uprooting during this era of social change, particularly as agriculture became industrialised.◆

startled her" (8); in a wedding carriage which sounds brutal and punitive – "It had stout wheel-spokes, and heavy felloes, a great curved bed, immense straps and springs, and a pole like a battering ram" (33); and set to work on the "tyrant" (47), the threshing machine which shakes her into a "stupefied reverie in which her arms worked on independently of her consciousness". (48)

"Life is movement," says Tanner, "and movement leads to confusion." Yet Tess is bound to keep moving, because she has no home. Uprooted, forced on to the road, ejected from houses, knocking on doors which remain closed to her: we see her becoming exhausted and helpless, and then being bundled off to a boarding house by Alec. When, finally, she is with Angel, it is as if she has almost given up the struggle to be human: he realizes that she "had spiritually ceased to recognize the body before him as hers – allowing it to drift, like a corpse upon the current, in a direction dissociated from its living will". (55) Tess has been so disturbed by irregularities of motion, so pulled in different directions, that she is already half dead.

The idea of the earth as a controlling force is present in every aspect of the novel, from its imagery to its structure. From the small, fertile vale of Blackmoor where she is born, she moves to Talbothays dairy, "oozing fatness and warm ferments" – a sensual dream, a brief, delusory vision of paradise. After that come the starved uplands of

Flintcomb-Ash with what Dorothy Van Ghent calls

> the ironic mimicry of the organs of generation, "myriads of loose white flints in bulbous, cusped and phallic shapes", and the dun consuming ruin of the swede field – the mockery of impotence, the exile.

It is as if the earth itself is punishing Tess:

> schematically simplified, the signifying form of the Tess-universe is the tragic heroism and tragic ineffectuality of [moral] consciousness in an antagonistic earth where events shape themselves by accident rather than by moral design ...

The coincidences of the plot reflect the antagonism

HARDY AND THE LEFT

Like most of us, critics often see what they want to see. In the 1950s, for example, left-wing academics emphasized the social aspects of Tess. The well- known Marxist, Arnold Kettle, decided that whatever Hardy might say about the novel's concern with a "pure woman", it was in fact about "the destruction of the English peasantry". *Tess* is the tragic story of the disintegration of the "old yeoman class" and Tess herself is "the symbol" of their destruction. When Joan Durbeyfield dresses her up in her working

of the earth. To some of the characters in the novel, these coincidences and mishaps are explained by folklore, magic and fatalism – a means of making sense of a world in which there are no rational explanations for what happens. When Tess first leaves Alec's house, a thorn from a rose pricks her chin. "Like all the cottagers in Blackmoor Vale, Tess was steeped in fancies and prefigurative superstitions; she thought this an ill omen..." (6) When the butter-making proves troublesome at Talbothays, dairyman Crick wonders if it means someone in the house is in love. A cock crows ominously on the afternoon of Tess's wedding. On making her fruitless quest to see Angel's parents, Tess sees

a piece of blood-stained paper, caught up from

clothes to go to Trantridge,

the moment is symbolic. Tess, prepared to become, since change she must, a worker, is handed over by her mother to the life and the mercies of the ruling class.

Her struggle to maintain her self-respect is hopeless: Angel, her supposed rescuer, turns out to be not just a prig and a hypocrite "but a snob as well". She becomes more and more degraded until forced on to the threshing machine at Flintcomb-Ash, "the symbol of the dehumanised relationships of the new capitalist farms". Kettle dismisses as fanciful the notion that Tess might be a victim of metaphysical fate. The novel, he says, reflects "no pretentious philosophy of fatality but a bitter recalling of the actual fate of millions of working women".

some meat-buyer's dust-heap, beat up and down
the road without the gate; too flimsy to rest, too
heavy to fly away; and a few straws kept it
company. (44)

It is another omen: Tess, too, is blood-stained and
forced to "beat up and down the road"; she, like the
paper, is too flimsy to rest, too heavy to fly away.
(There is an echo here of the dying Mrs Yeobright's
envy of the heron in *The Return of the Native*: "Up in
the zenith where he was seemed a free and happy
place, away from all contact with the earthly ball to
which she was pinioned; and she wished that she
could arise uncrushed from its surface and fly as he
flew then." (4/6))

The omens and the magic, the insistent use of the
colour red, the constant dwelling on the sun, the

Kettle later admitted that his assessment was somewhat one-sided, and another left-wing critic, Raymond Williams, argued (in 1964 and 1970) that changes to the rural society in fact came as much from within as from without. Another left-wing critic, Douglas Brown, a contemporary of Kettle's, charts the decline of agriculture in the late 19th century, noting the effects of such influences as industrialisation, free trade, poor harvests and the imports of cheap food. *Tess* shows "the agricultural community in its moment of ruin". The novel dramatises Tess's defeat. It is the defeat of "the country girl and representative of an ancient country line, and her ruin by the economic and spiritual invaders of country life."◆

endless movement – all reinforce Hardy's vision in *Tess* of an implacable, hostile earth which seems to have its own intentions and where unhappy accidents, coincidental though they may seem, are the rule rather than the exception. Hardy was "The Laureate of Sod's Law": what can go wrong will go wrong. Sometimes it appears as if his characters are sentient puppets in a cosmic Theatre of Cruelty; he suggests that the conditions under which consciousness has come into being are so overwhelmingly adverse that, if there is a dramatist behind the drama, his interest can only be in the creation of suffering. The tragedy of Tess and Angel is no mere accidental drama: "All the while they were converging, under an irresistible law, as surely as two streams in one vale." (20) And even Tess's frightful fate is set in context: she sees birds at Flintcomb-Ash "which had witnessed scenes of cataclysmal horror – of a magnitude such as no human being had ever conceived". (43) Hardy's physical awareness of things, says John Bayley, "was as strong as his sense of disquiet, amounting to incredulity, at the thought of the world they existed in".

How convincing is the climax of *Tess*?

In his fine study of Hardy, *The Great Web* (1974), Ian Gregor argues that Tess reveals "the endurance, the patience and the forgiveness of which the human spirit is capable". The spirit of the murdered Alec might be inclined to disagree. As with the other crises in the novel, we learn little about what actually happens, perhaps because it wouldn't have suited Hardy's purpose to tell us much. Just as to have shown Tess actually collaborating with Alec in acts of sexual gratification (even if she experienced no gratification herself) would have damaged Hardy's endeavour to present "faithfully" a "pure" woman, so to have depicted her carrying out an act of violent murder would have shaken our faith in a character supposedly so gentle and self-sacrificing. Hardy might respond that Tess is driven to distraction by Angel's arrival; also that she has shown previously that she could rebuke Alec in anger and even strike him hard enough to draw blood, as she did with her glove. Hardy told an interviewer that the stabbing was the logical outcome of "the hereditary quality" (presumably of aggressive pride) in Tess; but heredity is no defence in law.

In describing what happens, Hardy manipulates our response in his heroine's favour more by what is left out than by what is told. Mrs Brooks, the landlady at The Herons, hears "unusual sounds" coming from the apartment which Angel and Tess are renting; she looks through the keyhole, sees Tess in distress at the breakfast table, and hears her berate herself at length (in "a dirge rather than a soliloquy" (56)) for surrendering a second time to Alec's "cruel persuasions". Mrs Brooks hears "more and sharper words from the man", then "a sudden rustle". Soon after this, Tess hurries away from the inn, dressed in black. Alec's body is discovered on the bed, stabbed through the heart. Tess's subsequent explanation to Angel is brief and not very satisfactory:

> "But how do you mean – you have killed him?"
> "I mean that I have," she murmured in a reverie.
> "What, bodily? Is he dead?"
> "Yes. He heard me crying about you, and he bitterly taunted me; and called you by a foul name; and then I did it. My heart could not bear it. He had nagged me about you before. And then I dressed myself and came away to find you." (57)

We are given no details of the trial, moving straight from her arrest at Stonehenge to her execution at Wintoncester Gaol. In court, Mrs Brooks might have repeated her statement that Alec said something "sharp" – "bitterly taunted" is perhaps an overstatement – but that, and calling Angel "a foul name", hardly justify murder. Tess must have picked up the carving knife from the breakfast table, says John Sutherland,

> walked all the way across the length of the living room to the bed on which Alec was still lying, and stabbed him through the heart. One precisely aimed stroke has killed him. It is hard to imagine how this could be done – given Alec's superior strength and agility – unless Tess waited until he relapsed into sleep, as people do before breakfast. An awake Alec would hardly watch Tess stalking towards him with an upraised knife without raising a hand to defend himself or shifting his torso away from the path of the murder weapon.

Defence counsel might have argued that Tess had suffered abuse from her former lover, though there is no evidence he ever strikes or beats her, but no jury would be as lenient as the literary critics. Here is James Gibson summarizing Chapter 56:

> The landlady of the lodging house is curious – hears Tess moaning in her room and sharp words – she sees Tess leaving the house and then a red spot on the ceiling – Alec is dead.

"Alec is murdered", would be truer to the facts. Hardy's rhetoric, says Sutherland, allows the critic to overlook the simple wrongness of Tess's act, and mask it in neutral phraseology more appropriate to suicide or death by natural causes than homicide. The holes in Hardy's account allow us to jump to conclusions ("Alec is a rapist who gets what's coming to him") and sanction such exonerating imagery as Tony Tanner's: "Tess is gradually crucified on the oppugnant ironies of circumstance and existence itself." On objective legal grounds, one might retort, Tess deserves crucifixion rather more than do the two thieves and their famous companion.

What this account makes plain is the difficulties of treating *Tess* as a purely realistic narrative. Critics like Dorothy Van Ghent and Tony Tanner stress the emphasis on symbolism; Tess is often seen as an Everywoman figure, standing for femininity itself, her sexual body and her working body both vulnerable to exploitation by men (whether Alec, Angel or Famer Groby). Claire Tomalin describes her as an "emblematic figure": dancing on the green in a white dress in spring, at the dairy in the summer where everything is lush, at winter work in "colourless fields", sheltering among wounded pheasants whose plight, as Tomalin says, "mirrors hers". Irving Howe distinguishes her from Sue Bridehead in *Jude the Obscure*: whereas Sue, wilful and headstrong, "anticipates the modern cult of personality", Tess "represents something more deeply rooted in the substance of instinctual life": she is not "gratuitously restless or neurotically bored" (like Sue) but "spontaneously committed to the most fundamental needs of human existence". She "comes to seem for us the potential of what life could be, just as what happens to her signifies what life too often becomes".

In the 1980s deconstructionists went further, seeing the text as wholly ambiguous and open to all kinds of interpretations. The American critic J. Hillis Miller, for example, sees it as a narrative full of "blank spaces" where we are not told what has really happened. The reader must therefore "execute" what Hillis Miller calls "a lateral dance of interpretation" to explain any given passage.

Deconstructing *Tess* to this extent, however, seems neither helpful nor necessary. It may be true that the narrative is full of "blank spaces", but the impression of the world it leaves us with is abundantly clear and doesn't need a "lateral dance of interpretation" to make sense of it. This is not to say that it is scrupulously realistic; as we have already noted, it is far from it. To Hardy, a novel of scrupulous realism would have been a contradiction in terms; he saw life as too disordered, too chaotic; fiction to him was a way of seeing; his vision, ultimately, a poetic one. "Almost, it is necessary for [incidents like the one at Stonehenge] to be unrealistic," says John

Holloway, "in order that their other dimension of meaning, their relevance to the larger rhythms of the work, shall transpire." To Hardy, the killing of Alec, and Tess's subsequent, equally melodramatic capture at Stonehenge had symbolic, thematic and ironic aptness; they were psychologically justified, and they were central to the view of the world he was trying to convey in the novel.

Did a President of the Immortals sport with Tess?

Hardy's non-fictional pronouncements are often strongly defensive, as are these on *Tess*:

> The novel was intended to be neither didactic nor aggressive, but in the scenic parts to be representative simply, and in the contemplative to be oftener charged with impressions than with convictions...

He is partly right. Dorothy Van Ghent has warned against mistaking the "bits of philosophic adhesive tape" in the novel, "rather dampened and rumpled by time, for the deeply animated vision of experience" it contains. Yet if certain ideas are recurrent and vigorous in an author's fictional output, they form a significant part of the imaginative identity of that output, and this is undoubtedly the case with Hardy's work. His most famous and controversial judgement comes a few lines before the end, when, after noting the black flag which confirms Tess's death, the narrator says:

> *"Justice" was done, and the President of the Immortals, in Æschylean phrase, had ended his sport with Tess. (59)*

By putting "Justice" in ironic quotation-marks, Hardy declares his opposition to the judgement that Tess deserves the death-sentence; and, by apparently implying that Tess has been cruelly treated by some form of deity, he appears to express antitheism, the postulation of a hostile divine force. Among the early critics shocked by this was Andrew Lang, who wrote in dismay in the *New Review*: "If there be a God, who can seriously think of him as a malicious fiend?"

Hardy claimed that the critics had naïvely misinterpreted a poetic figure of speech; he was not really imputing cruelty to a "man-shaped tribal god". Inconsistently, he said that his idea had previously been expressed by Gloucester in *King Lear*: "As flies to wanton boys are we to the gods: / They kill us for their sport."

Yet the phrase from Æschylus's *Prometheus Bound* sums up quite aptly the impression created by Hardy's story.* Tess's bad luck is recurrent and extreme, and suggests that she has been the victim not only of human agency but of some greater force: notions of a hostile "supreme Mover" are present in the novel, and Hardy's theoretical distinction between "impressions" and "convictions" can scarcely disguise the intensity of his theological and moral indignation.

This indignation was at work when Hardy rewrote the last paragraph so that the sentence about "the President of the Immortals" replaced the original serial version: "Time, the Arch-Satirist, had had his joke out with Tess." "Time" lacks the theological animus imparted by the revision. And the bitterness of the revision is in line with other reflections in the novel casting doubt on the idea of a benign God, such as those accompanying Tess's violation (when God or a god is perhaps "in a journey, or he was sleeping") and Angel's attraction to her (when we are told that her very consciousness was "vouchsafed to Tess by an unsympathetic First Cause" (25)). Angel himself speaks of "mediæval times, when faith was a living thing" (17), implying that it has been dying since then.

In the vivid passage in which Tess, fearful of

*In *The Mayor of Casterbridge,* he asserts that Michael Henchard gave up his struggle because the odds were fixed against him by "that ingenious machinery contrived by the gods for reducing human possibilities of amelioration to a minimum". (44)

Hell, seeks advice about baptizing her baby, the narrator notes that the clergyman has retained some relics of nobler impulses "after ten years of endeavour to graft technical belief on actual scepticism": "The man and the ecclesiastic fought within him, and the victory fell to the man." (14) In the end, though, the clergyman won't help, and Tess is forced to carry out the ceremony herself.

> *So the baby was carried in a small deal box, under an ancient woman's shawl, to the churchyard that night, and buried by lantern-light, at the cost of a shilling and a pint of beer to the sexton, in that shabby corner of God's allotment where He lets the nettles grow, and where all unbaptized infants, notorious drunkards, suicides, and others of the conjecturally damned are laid.*

This is Hardy at his best – a brilliant sentence, alive with controlled anger. It begins, as David Lodge has noted, with a "subdued literal description" of the child's burial. A hint of irony appears in the shilling and the pint of beer; this becomes overt when the narrator moves from impersonal narration to comment: "that shabby corner of God's allotment where He lets the nettles grow". Here, God is presented "as a cynically careless smallholder", a stroke particularly appropriate given the agrarian background to the story. The irony is sustained and intensified, says Lodge,

> in the conclusion of the sentence, in the grouping of the unbaptized infants with drunkards and suicides, and in the juxtaposition of the cool "conjecturally" with the uncompromising "damned", which effectively shocks us into awareness of the arrogance and inhumanity of presuming to forecast the eternal destiny of souls.

This passage, like others in the narrative, suggest that formalised Christianity has propagated a morality which is too severe and repressive. Hardy discriminates: Angel's pious parents are, if blinkered, nevertheless good people, capable of welcoming a "fallen woman"; his brothers, on the other hand, are depicted as weak creatures of conventional piety. While Tess's own Christianity, as we have suggested, never seems entirely plausible, she seems in the novel to outgrow Christian metaphysics but not Christian ethics: she waveringly loses belief in a supernatural deity, while retaining belief in the spirit of Christ's Sermon on the Mount (Matthew, Chapters 5-7). Alec's surprising phase of faith is destroyed partly by a "merciless syllogism" from Tess. Though not specified, the syllogism is probably of this kind: "God is, reputedly, both good and omnipotent. But evil flourishes on earth. Therefore, if God is good, He is not omnipotent; or, if omnipotent, He is not good." (Hardy once told a correspondent that Nature is either "blind and not a judge of her actions" or "an automaton, and unable to control them".) Near the end of her life, Tess thinks of sharing Angel with 'Liza-Lu "when we are spirits", but Angel accentuates her distress by denying her the prospect of such immortality.

As for Angel himself: whereas Browning's Pippa had sung "God's in his heaven – / All's right with the world!", he thinks "God's *not* in his heaven; all's *wrong* with the world!". This is the impression the novel gives, though it also, intermittently, gives the impression that there may be a "First Cause", "Will", or cosmic force which is uncaring and, at times, actively cruel. This uncertainty about

HARDY AND RELIGION

Agnosticism, the belief that humans cannot know whether there is or is not a God, has been available in various forms since ancient times. It may be traced, for example, to the radical scepticism of Pyrrho of Elis (circa 360-272 BC). The term "agnosticism" itself (derived from the Greek *a*, not, and *gnostikos*, good at knowing) was probably first coined in 1869 by Thomas Huxley, "Darwin's bulldog", whom Hardy met and praised: his essays are cited in *Tess*. An atheist asserts that there is no God, while the antitheist asserts that

whether human actions were simply random or controlled by some kind of supernatural being was widespread in the late 19th century. Fitzgerald's Omar Khayyám, Swinburne, Conrad and even Bertrand Russell all expressed it. Russell's essay, "The Free Man's Worship" (1903) says that though there are no supernatural beings, humans exist "amid hostile forces" and must "struggle with the powers of darkness": phrases which surely bring supernatural agencies to mind. In the imagination even of the sceptic, religious imagery often retained its potency.

Tess of the d'Urbervilles offers little indication of the notion expressed by Hardy in various poems and in *The Dynasts*, that the "First Cause", the creating "Will", might eventually evolve into consciousness, recognise what it has done, and

God (or a god) exists but is uncaring or malevolent instead of benevolent. Hardy claimed to be "a harmless agnostic", but that claim was repeatedly belied by the vigour with which he voiced atheistic and antitheistic sentiments. Indeed, the context of his phrase aptly illustrates this point:

To cry out in a passionate poem that (for instance) the Supreme Mover or Movers, the Prime Force or Forces, must be either limited in power, unknowing, or cruel – which is obvious enough, and has been for centuries – will cause them [i.e. "the vast body of men"] merely a shake of the head; but to put it in argumentative prose will make them sneer, or foam, and set all the literary contortionists jumping upon me, a harmless agnostic, as if I were a clamorous atheist,

clean up out the mess it has made on earth:

Consciousness the Will informing, till
It fashion all things fair!

In *Tess*, Hardy displays a detailed familiarity not just with the Bible and its interpreters, and with classical mythology, but with philosophers ancient and modern. Among the strongest influences was Arthur Schopenhauer, who died in 1860 and whose works were carefully annotated by Hardy. The most pessimistic of philosophers, Schopenhauer claimed that the universe is permeated by a "will" or life-force which generates human beings, who are destined to suffer; the wise person seeks detachment from this futile vitality. Life, Schopenhauer alleged, may be deemed "an

which in their crass illiteracy they seem to think is the same thing.

There, in the act of terming himself an agnostic and not an atheist, he concedes that the ideas which he wishes to "cry out" include the idea that "the Supreme Mover" is not omnipotent, omniscient and loving (as Christians maintain) but, on the contrary, "either limited in power, unknowing, or cruel"

– a range which includes the antitheistic.

Certainly, hostile critics seized indignantly on that sardonic declaration near the end of the novel about the "President of the Immortals" ending "his sport" with Tess. Hardy claimed that the critics had naïvely misinterpreted a poetic figure of speech; he was being metaphorical, and they were taking him too literally.◆

Natassja Kinski in Roman Polanksi's 1979 Tess

unprofitable episode, disturbing the blessed calm of non-existence"; and children resemble "innocent prisoners, condemned, not to death, but to life", so that truly rational adults would not produce offspring. Buddhism, by showing the kinship of humans with animals, was morally superior to Christianity.

Tess is permeated by Schopenhauer's ideas: we recall the narrator's comment on "the chronic melancholy" which accompanies "the decline of belief in a beneficent Power" (18); Tess's notion that we live on a blighted star; her pessimistic intuition, which Angel terms "the ache of modernism" (19); and the sense that the Durbeyfields' children have unthinkingly been born into a vale of sorrows, so that Tess is "a Malthusian" (5) – i.e. one who, like Thomas Malthus, commends control of the birth-rate. Even the renunciative outlook of Angel's father, we are told, has "cousinship with that of Schopenhauer". In the novel, Schopenhauer is also linked to a poet whom Hardy admired, Giacomo Leopardi; and, significantly, Leopardi's canzone *Bruto minore* (1821) suggests that the gods play arbitrary games with hapless human beings, whose lives are blighted by reason.

Hardy, a supporter of the Royal Society for the Prevention of Cruelty to Animals, would have appreciated Schopenhauer's sympathy with animals; he felt that subsequent Darwinism, by specifying our descent from "a hairy quadruped", implied that we should be more considerate to our fellow-creatures. Prince's death is treated with great sensitivity; Tess, appalled to find herself in a grove full of dying birds (the victims of a callous shooting-party), puts the wounded creatures out of their misery.

The narrator of *Tess* endorses various New Testament values (love, charity, kindness, forgiveness as of the "woman taken in adultery"), though the Testament's "redemptive theolatry" is condemned, and Christian theology treated as outmoded. That creed "had served mankind well in its time" (12), but makes Tess fear that her baby will go to Hell and be tormented by Satan.

Tensions and paradoxes abound in the novel. Sometimes it implies that sombre Christianity (with "the pale Galilean") has historically displaced radiant Hellenism, which celebrated beauty and what the poet Matthew Arnold called "spontaneity of consciousness". Nevertheless, the loss of Christian faith is said to induce melancholy. Life is a vale of sorrows, but the "tendency to find sweet pleasure somewhere... pervades all life". (16) Tess cannot help having an "appetite for joy" (30); like many of Hardy's characters, she is aware of a capacity for bliss in herself which cannot be satisfied in the wearisome conditions of day-to-day living. As we look back on these contrasting views, we may say, with the narrator, "such is human inconsistency". (15)

There are moral judgements in *Tess* which are indeed inconsistent and contradictory, but the narrative as a whole implies a complex moral outlook which is sufficiently coherent. It is as though, as the story proceeds, several commentators are being provoked to offer widely-ranging interpretations. Though one is merely an agnostic, another is the antitheist who shakes a fist at a "President of the Immortals" – a poetic personification shimmeringly evoking an objective superhuman referent, whether secular (the cosmic creative process) or supernatural (that "Supreme Mover"). Arguably, provocative variety is preferable to predictable uniformity. Hardy would have agreed with Keats: a good poet should be content with uncertainties.

What does *Tess* tell us about human consciousness?

Although *Tess*, like all Hardy's novels, is full of coincidences, the main developments – Tess's deflowering, her rejection by Angel, the murder of Alec – are all psychologically motivated. Arguably, coincidence and chance, to Hardy, are consistent with the lack of understanding between people, the way they are internally divided, the arbitrariness of life, human helplessness and the likely failure of human relationships. Passionate love in Hardy's work often exists when there are objects to prevent its fulfilment; the sexual instinct in his novels often leads to misery.

This is partly because of the way we see what we want to see; and what we see in those we love, Hardy suggests, is something they can't live up to, something that doesn't, and can't, exist. For Angel, Tess before her confession is a goddess or "a visionary essence of woman" (20); for Tess, Angel seems similarly divine: "he was... godlike in her eyes". (29) The idea that what we see depends on our state of mind recurs in the novel: "the world is only a psychological phenomenon" (13), says the narrator early on, and the novel demonstrates in all kinds of ways the impossibility of a fully objective and detached view of life. To the drinkers at Rolliver's, in their intoxicated state,

> *the chamber and its furniture grew more and more dignified and luxurious; the shawl hanging at the window took upon itself the richness of tapestry; the brass handles of the chest of drawers were as golden knockers; and the carved bed-posts seemed to have some kinship with the magnificent pillars of Solomon's temple. (4)*

After Tess's confession, "external things seemed to suffer transmutation":

The fire in the grate looked impish –
demoniacally funny, as if it did not care in the
least about her strait. The fender grinned idly, as
if it too did not care. (35)

And Angel, instead of seeing a goddess, sees
Tess's white face: "her cheek was flaccid, her
mouth had almost the aspect of a little round
hole". (35) The novel, says Dale Kramer, shows
us the intense subjectivity of human experience.
Tess feels she is "not an existence, an experience, a
passion, a structure of sensations, to anybody but
herself". To the rest of mankind she is "only a
passing thought". (14) Kramer believes that "the
unique quality" of the tragedy is that within the
pages of the novel Tess is tragic only to herself.
"To others, she is a puzzling daughter, a temptingly
lovely girl and woman, an image of purity, a fallen
woman..."

The isolation of individual consciousness – and
what Kramer deems a denial of objective truth – is
emphasized in the novel by the dream-like aura of
many scenes. There is the "mist of yellow
radiance" (10) at the Chaseborough dance, and the
"floating pollen" (19) in the garden where Tess
listens to Angel's flute. Before her marriage, Tess
moves about "in a mental cloud of mental
idealities" (33); afterwards Angel sleepwalks with
her in his arms. Her agonised wanderings after
Angel leaves for Brazil, partake, as Kramer puts it,

"of the quality of dream persecution". The man operating the steam engine which tyrannizes Tess at Flintcomb-Ash is like a figure from a nightmare. "A little way off was another indistinct figure; this one black... He was in the agricultural world, but not of it. He served fire and smoke."(47) It is an image echoed by Alec's subsequent appearance to Tess, where he appears like a pursuing devil amidst smouldering fires and smoke. Dream-like, too, is the scene where Angel finds Tess in a Bournemouth boarding house: in a kind of trance he "finds" she has left the room, then he "finds" himself in the street.

Hardy often reminds us that from almost every point of view except her own Tess is insignificant. She feels "akin to the landscape" (16), for example, as she descends to the Valley of the Dairies while in fact she is "of no more consequence than... a fly on a billiard table". But to Tess herself, her experience is the only thing that matters. Angel himself realises this after their marriage:

[She] was no insignificant creature to toy with and dismiss; but a woman living her precious life... Upon her sensations the whole world depended to Tess... The universe itself only came into being for Tess on the particular day in the particular year in which she was born. (25)

Conversely, the new residents at the Durbeyfield

CRITICS ON *TESS*

66 Tess of the d'Urbervilles *is an extraordinarily beautiful book, as well as an extraordinarily moving one.* 99
A. Alvarez, 1978

66 *The final impression is of a loving and lovable person, a woman of vibrant life and of an immense potential for happiness and for doing good[,] who is destroyed by a life-denying system, by false values, and by the cruelty of the two men in her life.* 99 James Gibson, 1993

66 *A "tragic masterpiece" comparable with* King Lear *and* Macbeth. *"Powerful and strange in design, splendid and terrible in execution, this story brands itself upon the mind as with the touch of incandescent iron.* 99
William Watson in The Academy, 1892

66 *[The] combination of sexual vigour and moral rigour... makes Tess not just one of the greatest but also one of the strongest women in the annals of English literature.* 99
Rosemarie Morgan, 1988

66 *[Tess] is Hardy's greatest tribute to the possibilities of human existence, for [she] is one of the greatest triumphs of civilisation: a natural girl."* 99
Irving Howe, 1967

66 *Tess has no 'character' at all: she is only what others construct her as... and so is herself merely a 'series of seemings'... This is at once a radical subversion of the liberal-bourgeois conception of the individual and of the humanist-realist conception of 'character'; and... it is precisely related to class/gender alienation.* 99
Peter Widdowson, 1989, using the text to support traditional deconstructive and Marxist notions

cottage, after Tess's family has left, "walked about the garden paths with thoughts of their own concerns entirely uppermost" and the birds go on singing "as if they thought there was nobody missing in particular". (54) Tess's baby, Sorrow, was

a waif to whom eternal Time had been a matter of days merely, who knew not that such things as years and centuries ever were; to whom the cottage interior was the universe, the week's weather climate, new-born babyhood human existence, and the instinct to suck human knowledge. (14)

The "capability of creating tragedy", opines Kramer, "resides only in the character who feels the tragedy".

Trapped in their subjective worlds, Tess and Angel see the world quite differently; even had they met before she met Alec, the relationship would still have been doomed. Years after the novel had been published, Hardy was asked what might have happened if the pair had met earlier: he said Angel would quickly have tired of Tess; the disparity between them, in terms of class and outlook, was too great.

"The 'poetry' of Tess herself has its light put out by her confession, for the novel as well as for Clare," says John Bayley. "She has lost her power to enchant; her 'face is made bare', as in the verse of

Swinburne which Hardy suddenly inserts; she becomes 'as a tale that is told'."

Our sympathy for her after this increases, but so does her own sense of alienation. This sense has always been there. Despite her thirst for happiness, she knows what she finds with Angel can't last. At first her love for him sustains her:

> *it enveloped her as a photosphere, irradiated her into forgetfulness of her past sorrows, keeping back the gloomy spectres that would persist in their attempts to touch her – doubt, fear, moodiness, care, shame. She knew they were waiting like wolves outside the circumscribing light, but she had long spells of power to keep them in hungry subjection there... She walked in brightness, but she knew that in the background those shapes of darkness were always spread. (31)*

This is quintessential Hardy; it condenses a whole vision of existence, like the extraordinary scene in *The Return of the Native* where Clym and the Reddleman sit gambling amidst the darkness in a tiny circle of light created by some glow worms they have gathered: "Amid the soft juicy vegetation ... and the uninhabited solitude, intruded the chink of guineas, the rattle of dice, the exclamations of the reckless players." (3/8)

Tess tries to fit into life – to feel that she is somehow unique – but she can't. Early on she is struck by the thought that "thousands of others" (19) have lived lives just like hers. When her baby dies she wonders when her own "death day" will be – "a day which lay sly and unseen among all the other days of the year" (15) – and frequently longs to escape her earthly existence. At Talbothays she says one day: "I do know that our souls can be made to go outside our bodies when we are alive." (18) Her method is to fix the mind on a remote star and "you will soon find you are hundreds and hundreds o' miles away from your body, which you don't seem to want at all". (18) Like Hardy's other major characters, she is a potential suicide. Rejected by Angel, she asks him if she can throw herself in the river. Shortly afterwards, the two figures are seen "walking very slowly without converse, as in a funeral procession". (35) The scene is one Hardy recreates in his poem, "Beyond the Last Lamp":

Moving slowly, moving sadly
That mysterious tragic pair...

Many of Hardy's most striking visual moments concern death, or impending doom: Mrs Yeobright in *The Return of the Native*, watching the struggling ants below her and the heron above, before she dies from an adder's bite; Troy, in *Far from the Madding Crowd*, arranging flowers on Fanny's grave which are washed away by water from a "grinning" church gargoyle; or Michael Henchard in *The Mayor of Casterbridge* seeing his effigy float down a river. The same is true of *Tess*. Scene after scene offers some *memento mori*, a reminder of death. The horse is killed; Tess's child dies and, later, so does her father; Retty Pridde attempts suicide; Angel nearly dies abroad. Three times, before Stonehenge, Tess is associated with tombs. After leaving Alec for the first time, and returning home, she wakes one morning feeling so depressed that "she could have hidden herself in a tomb". (13) On her wedding night, Angel sleep-walks into her room, saying "Dead, dead, dead! ... My wife – dead, dead!" (37) He takes her in his arms, carrying her across a river : Tess is tempted to jog him so that he drops her, but Angel, able to avoid the turbulent waters as he is able to suppress passion, lays her in "an empty stone coffin" in the "ruined choir". ("He encoffins the sexual instinct," says Tony Tanner.) Tess's family are desperate, and they take refuge in the church containing the family vaults. It is here that Alec plays his malicious trick, leaping out from a tomb. Pursued by Alec, rejected by Angel, Tess bends down at her ancestors' vault and whispers: "Why am I on the wrong side of this door?" (52)

Hardy's pessimism shapes *Tess*. While humanist critics like Roy Morrell have sought to show that in fact he is not a pessimist and not a determinist, and that his characters, far from being pawns in the hands of hostile Nature, shape their own destinies, the argument is less than convincing. Hardy may have been always on the look-out for signs that humanity was improving; if so. he failed to find them: "After two thousand years of mass / We've got as far as poison-gas," he wrote in his poem "Christmas: 1924".

"What is the intensely maturing experience of which Hardy's modern man is most sensible?" asked Philip Larkin.

> In my view it is suffering, or sadness, and extended consideration of the centrality of suffering in Hardy's work should be the first duty of the true critic...

It is a simple point which some critics, in their anxiety to see Hardy as proto-feminist, or social critic, or modernist, or humanist, fail to stress. Hardy, as Larkin says, was peculiarly well-equipped to perceive "the melancholy, the misfortunate, the frustrating, the failing elements of life". Like Little Father Time in *Jude the Obscure*, it could be said of him that he would like the flowers very much if he didn't keep thinking they would all be withered in a few days. "Tragedy is true guise,/Comedy lies," Hardy once wrote. In *Jude the Obscure*, his last novel, Jude reflects that "at the framing of the terrestrial conditions there seemed never to have been contemplated such a development of emotional perceptiveness as that reached by thinking and educated humanity." (6/3) "Oh, the cruelty of putting me into this ill-conceived world," rages Eustacia in *The Return of the Native*. (5/7) "Oh! Why were we given hungry hearts and wild desires if we have to live in a world like this," cries Felice Charmond in *The Woodlanders*. (27)

Hardy believed that any developed consciousness was bound to suffer, and that awareness of suffering and the causes of pain was the sign of a sensitive nature. "A woeful fact [is] that the human race is too extremely developed for its corporeal conditions," he noted in 1889. "This planet does not supply the materials for happiness to higher existences." Women, he believed, were more sensitive than men, and prone to suffer more. And of Hardy's women, none suffers more than his Tess: she was, in a sense, a symbol of his vision of the world.

A SHORT CHRONOLOGY

1840 Born in Higher Bockhampton near Dorchester, first of four children of Thomas Hardy, a builder and stonemason, and his wife Jemima.

1850 His serious schooldays begin when he is enrolled into a school set up in Dorchester by Isaac Last, a clever Noncomformist headmaster. Learns Latin and – a "born bookworm", as he called himself – reads voraciously.

1856 Becomes an apprentice to the Dorchester architect, John Hicks. Continues his studies at home and begins to learn Greek.

1856 Aged 16, joins the crowds to see Martha Browne hanged for murder at Dorchester Gaol. He never forgot the experience. "I am ashamed to say I saw her hanged," he wrote in a letter when he was an old man; his only excuse was he was young, he added. "I remember what a fine figure she showed against the sky as she hung in the misty rain, and how the tight black silk gown set off her shape as she wheeled half-round and back."

1862 Moves to London to work for a distinguished architect, Arthur Blomfield.

1867 Begins work on his first (unpublished) novel, *The Poor Man and the Lady*.

1870 Horace Moule, the son of a minister and Hardy's closest and most influential childhood friend, commits suicide by cutting his throat. He was a depressive. "Never again would Hardy have a friend who held his heart so wholly," writes Claire Tomalin. Meets Emma Gifford, his future wife, while restoring St Juliot's church in north Cornwall.

1871 *Desperate Remedies* published.

1874 *Far from the Madding Crowd* serialised and published as a book, a year after the publication of *A Pair of Blue Eyes*. Marries Emma at St Peter's, Paddington. The honeymoon is spent in France.

1878 *The Return of the Native*. Though not really a clubbable man, he joins the Savile Club. Later also becomes a member of the Athenæum. As his fame spreads, he becomes an established figure in the literary world, meeting Henry James, Matthew Arnold, Tennyson and Browning.

1885 The Hardys move into Max Gate, the house they have built in Dorset. *The Mayor of Casterbridge* completed.

1887 *The Woodlanders*.

1890 Visits Paris in August with his brother Henry to show him the sights. These included a visit to the Moulin Rouge to see the can-can performed, though he doesn't record his impressions of this. The passing of the US Copyright Act, as well as the success of *Tess*, makes Hardy rich. He buys two houses in Dorchester, one for his sisters, both now teaching there, and one as an investment.

1891 *Tess of the d'Urbervilles* published.

1895 *Jude the Obscure*. Heavily criticised for its radical views on marriage and Christianity. Some booksellers were said to have wrapped it in brown paper before selling it. "After verdicts from the press its next misfortune was to be burnt by a bishop [the Bishop of Wakefield], probably in his despair at not being able to burn me," Hardy later wrote. *Jude* was his last novel.

1907 Finishes *The Dynasts*.

1910 Awarded the Order of Merit by King George V.

1912 Emma Hardy dies at about 8am on November 27th. It is "the moment when Thomas Hardy became a great poet", says Claire Tomalin. Filled with sorrow and remorse for his coldness in the estrangement which had developed between them, he had her coffin placed at the foot of his bed, where it remained for three days and nights until the funeral.

1914 Marries Florence Dugdale at St Andrew's, Enfield, Middlesex.

1923 Augustus John's portrait of Hardy, showing a face "refined into an essence", as T.E. Lawrence put it. "I don't know whether that is how I look or not – but that is how I *feel*," said Hardy.

1919 Macmillan publish his *Collected Poems*, but his output remains prodigious and he publishes three further volumes of poetry.

1923 July. The Prince of Wales, on a tour of Somerset, Dorset and Wiltshire, has lunch with Hardy and Florence at Max Gate. A retinue of 13 have to be fed in the house, not counting the chauffeurs, while the grandees accompanying the Prince eat under trees in the garden. The Prince "did not pretend to have read anything by his host", says Claire Tomalin, and rural matters were probably discussed. The lunch went well. "I didn't fuss around him," Florence wrote afterwards, "and I think he was grateful. He made himself very much at home... He grew rather gay and jocular... I had been told he ate nothing." In fact he asked for a second helping of ham and finished up with "a glass of 40-year-old sherry" and a cigar.

1928 January 11, Hardy dies following a heart attack in the evening. Subsequently his ashes are interred in Westminster Abbey and his heart buried at Stinsford.

BIBLIOGRAPHY

Alvarez, A., "Introduction" to *Tess of the d'Urbervilles*, ed. David Skilton. Harmondsworth: Penguin, 1978.

Bayley, John, *An Essay on Hardy.* Cambridge: Cambridge U. P., 1978.

Boumelha, Penny, *Thomas Hardy and Women: Sexual Ideology and Narrative Form.* Brighton: Harvester, 1982.

Clarke, Graham (ed.), *Thomas Hardy: Critical Assessments* (4 vols.). Mountfield: Helm Information, 1993.

Gatrell, Simon, "Introduction" to *Tess of the d'Urbervilles*, ed. J. Grindle and S. Gatrell. Oxford: Oxford U. P., 1988.

Gibson, James, "Introduction" to *Tess of the d'Urbervilles*, ed. J. Gibson. London: Dent, 1984.

Gregor, Ian. *The Great Web: The Form of Hardy's Major Fiction.* London: Faber and Faber, 1974.

Howe, Irving, *Thomas Hardy.* London: Weidenfeld and Nicolson, 1968.

Irwin, Michael, *Reading Hardy's Landscapes.* Basingstoke: Macmillan, 2000.

Kramer, Dale, *Thomas Hardy: The Forms of Tragedy.* London: Macmillan, 1975.

Laird, J. T., *The Shaping of "Tess of the d'Urbervilles".* London: Oxford U. P., 1975.

Larkin, Philip, "Wanted: Good Hardy Critic" (1966) in *Required Writing: Miscellaneous Piece 1955-1982.* London: Faber and Faber, 1983.

Lodge, David, "Tess, Nature, and the Voices of Hardy" in *Language of Fiction.* London: Routledge & Kegan Paul, 1966.

Morgan, Rosemarie, *Women and Sexuality in the Novels of Thomas Hardy.* London and New York: Routledge, 1988.

Morrell, Roy, *Thomas Hardy: The Will and the Way.* Kuala Lumpur: Malaya U. P., 1965.

Sumner, Rosemary, *Thomas Hardy: Psychological Novelist.* London: Macmillan, 1981.

Sutherland, John, "Is Alec a Rapist?" in *Is Heathcliff a Murderer?: Puzzles in Nineteenth-Century Literature.* Oxford: Oxford U. P., 1996.

Tanner, Tony, "Colour and Movement in *Tess of the d'Urbervilles*": *Critical Quarterly* 10 (1968), 219-39.

Tomalin, Claire, *Thomas Hardy: The Time-Torn Man.* London: Penguin, 2006.

Van Ghent, Dorothy, *The English Novel: Form and Function.* New York: Holt, Rinehart & Winston, 1953.

INDEX

("ff." below means "and subsequent pages".)

First published in 2012 by
Connell Guides
Spye Arch House
Spye Park
Lacock
Chippenham
Wiltshire SN15 2PR

10 9 8 7 6 5 4 3 2 1

Picture credits:
p.9 © Lebrecht
p.45 © Bridgeman
p.53 © Getty
p.61 © British Library
p.71 © Illustrated London News Ltd/Mary Evans
p.113 © Alamy

A CIP catalogue record for this book is available
from the British Library.
ISBN 978-1-907776-09-0

Assistant Editor: Katie Sanderson
Typesetting: Katrina ffiske
Design © Nathan Burton
Printed in Great Britain by Butler Tanner and Dennis

www.connellguides.com